Sustainable Housing Projects

Implementing a Conceptual Approach

Sustainable Housing Projects

Implementing a Conceptual Approach

Ronald Rovers

With contributions from Frank Klinckenberg,
Piet Heijnen, Martin de Wit, Mieke Weterings, Adriaan Mels, Frans de Haas,
Martin Mooij, Kees Duijvestein, Ger de Vries, Tjerk Reijenga

Techne Press, Amsterdam

Colofon

Sustainable Housing Projects

Implementing a Conceptual Approach

Editor
Ronald Rovers

With contributions from
Frank Klinckenberg, Piet Heijnen, Martin de Wit,
Mieke Weterings, Adriaan Mels, Frans de Haas, Martin Mooij, Kees Duijvestein,
Ger de Vries and Tjerk Reijenga

ISBN 978-90-8594-020-3
Ecodesign, Sustainable Urban Design, Planning, Integrative Approach,
Sustainable Architecture, Environmental Building

Publisher
Techne Press, Amsterdam 2008
www. technepress.nl

Lay out
Roos Berendsen

This book has been prepared with the support of
Senter Novem, VROM and Wageningen University

Table of contents

Foreword

This book presents knowledge gained over the last 15 years developing new sustainable housing projects in the Netherlands. This development could be said to have started with the opening of Ecolonia in 1993, the first large-scale housing project demonstrating sustainable building. Many lessons have been learned and a great deal of experience has been gained since then.

Colleagues abroad have often asked about the Dutch experience and knowledge, but until now there was no comprehensive overview available in English. Eleven Dutch specialists in sustainable building, both practitioners and researchers, occasionally working together advising foreign projects, decided to collect and document their experience in a compact and accessible form.

The main aim of this book is to show the importance of not thinking in measures, but taking a conceptual approach, which leaves room for different solutions within a clear context of targets. A second objective is to show that important decisions have to be taken at the very first moment, before the architect draws the first line. The stakeholders should be aware of the targets and agree about them, thus avoiding making choices which limit possibilities later on, or can only be changed at high cost and effort.

Some topics have not been fully addressed in this book. These include spatial (building) planning, land management (for competing uses such as food, materials, biomass, housing, etc), transport, and social sustainability. It is also currently recognised that the existing building/housing stock is the most important topic to address if we are to reduce the environmental burden in an absolute way. Though this is referred to in this book, it requires a separate approach.

This publication has been put together in the hope that many more people can gain a better understanding of how we have managed so far in the Netherlands, bearing in mind that there is still a great deal to be done before a real shift towards balanced sustainability takes place.

Ronald Rovers - November 2007

Introduction

Sustainable building has been applied in the Netherlands for more than 15 years, with a first very visible milestone in 1993: the demonstration project *Ecolonia*. At that time, the general approach to sustainable building was to implement specific measures that would improve the performance of a building, and *Ecolonia* provided an overview of many measures and technologies. Since then, experience has led to the conclusion that implementing a 'concept' is a better approach than an uncoordinated collection of separate measures. The concept approach has been applied in projects as well as in other areas, such as municipal management strategies and national policies.

The rationale for sustainable building

Why has all this taken place? The number of reasons for sustainable building has only grown over the years. One of the first reasons was to limit the use of fossil-fuels, following the oil crisis of the early 70's. Air pollution, with its adverse impact on health, was the next, followed by political uncertainty in the world (and the trend towards self-sufficiency), and general concerns about limited global resources. In recent years, commercial opportunities (for renewable sources of energy and materials) have also become a factor for promoting sustainable building practices. At the moment, reports about the serious and direct effects of climate change are causing renewed interest in sustainability.

Definitions

One of the problems when one speaks of sustainable development and, more specifically, sustainable building, is how to define these terms: what is sustainable building? In different parts of the world, the concept is interpreted differently, and even experts use the term differently. In general, we can say that sustainable building involves the balanced uses of resources on a global scale (e.g., energy, materials, water, land). These physical elements are the most tangible: availability is limited, negative environmental impacts are well known, and there are clear strategies to reduce resource use (although so far these have only been implemented very partially). Human elements come next: healthy living conditions, comfort, and social and cultural adjustment to what people perceive as important in life, their needs and desires.

Sustainable building field
Source: Ronald Rovers

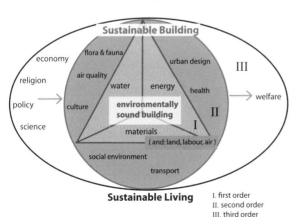

I. first order
II. second order
III. third order

Ecolonia project
Source: Ronald Rovers

All this has to be established within the national political context, with the economy as a regulating system, with research supporting solutions, and culture and sometimes religion as structuring framework. These three scales are sometimes summarised as 'ecology, sociology and economy,' or as 'people, planet, profit.'

This suggests that all three have the same level of importance. However, the physically available resources (energy, materials, clean water, clean air, land, etc.) set the limit on the material framework within which people can create their welfare, while the economic system (with profit as a part of it) has to facilitate this, but is not a goal in itself.

Structure of the book

The various issues of sustainable building are presented. Chapter 2 on Comfort and Climate describes the basic conditions required for human habitation in sheltered areas. Chapter 3 on Resources summarises the conditions imposed by an environmentally-sound approach. Chapter 4, Planning and Design, shows how both comfort and environmental conditions can be synthesised and applied to actual designs. But the book begins with a chapter describing the concept and the context of sustainable building, introducing the institutions in which the building and construction market has to operate and how such a framework can be developed to facilitate progress towards a truly sustainable approach.

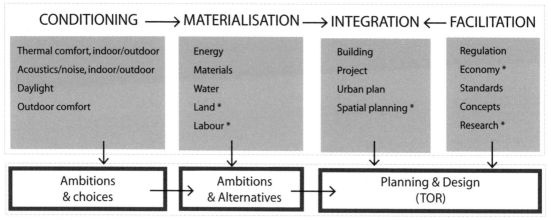

* Not included in this document

1 Sustainable Building: the concept and the context

A conceptual approach

In implementing sustainable building, the concepts approach has been shown to be of the utmost importance, since individual or separate measures often lead at best to less than optimum solutions, and sometimes even to the opposite, known as the 'rebound effect'. For example, the introduction of energy-efficient light bulbs has led to reduced energy demand for lighting in living rooms, but also to more lights and more usage hours (and therefore more fossil-fuel energy use) in other parts of homes, like gardens. Similarly, preventing air leakage in homes is one of the first effective measures that people can take, reducing ventilation losses and therefore energy consumption. But at the same time this can cause humidity problems in the building and poor air quality indoors. Reducing ventilation losses therefore has to be part of an overall concept of combined energy measures. Another example is when an inefficient local heating system is replaced by a highly efficient boiler heating system which supports the whole building. This can only be effective if the whole building/home is addressed in a total approach which combines heating, ventilation, insulation, heat loss, installations and the behaviour of the inhabitants. Likewise, when material use is reduced by eliminating the roof overhang, the demand for maintenance of the façades increases, resulting in a net increase in environmental pressure over the building's lifetime. And more recently other interrelated aspects have been discovered: drying laundry hanging indoors in winter (which is needed in colder climates) creates a lot of water vapour, increasing heat and ventilation demand. It has been shown that in many cases a clothes dryer is a better alternative environmentally when no unheated, naturally ventilated space such as an attic is available for drying. The concept approach does not stop at the building: the neighbourhood also needs to be included in developing a good concept, since a communal laundry shop may be even more effective, assuming that it is within a reasonable distance. These are all important aspects of planning and designing housing and neighbourhoods, and show the need for a conceptual approach. The same approach needs to be applied to materials, water, traffic and transport planning, and land use management, etc.

The concept approach sets an overall goal for a specific aspect and combines measures, technologies, design details, and management support to achieve a totality with optimum results. And, of course, a concept in one area also has to be evaluated in relation to those in other areas. In some cases the introduction of a

1 REDUCE NEED OF USE

2 USE RENEWABLE SOURCES

3 SUPPLY REMAINING NEEDS AS EFFICIENTLY AS POSSIBLE

measure in one concept can have an impact on the performance of another. For instance, insulation material reduces energy consumption (as part of an energy concept) but it increases the use of materials (in the materials concept). In this case, using recycled or renewable materials for insulation would be preferable, thus avoiding a rebound effect in material use caused by the energy concept.

Trias Ecologica

The *Trias Ecologica* has proven to be a useful three step strategy for developing sustainable and environmental concepts. This principle states that the first step is to reduce the need for or use of anything. The next step is to use renewable sources to meet the need. And if the first two steps are not sufficient, the third step can be applied: supply the remaining needs as efficiently as possible.

Applied to energy, this leads to a major reduction in demand (through insulation, efficient ventilation, daylight optimisation, etc.), the introduction of renewable energy sources (e.g., solar collectors, passive solar gains by design, solar electricity), and highly efficient use of fossil fuels to meet the remaining need. These steps need to be applied in that order. The same approach can be used for materials, water consumption, and even for maintenance or installations.

Closed cycle approach

By natural progression, the *Trias Ecologica* approach leads to a closed cycle approach, in which all needs are taken care of in step 1 and 2, and step 3 can then be eliminated. At that point, non-renewable resources are no longer needed, and there will be a balanced situation for the activity. It is not be possible to reach this optimum situation with an 'adding measures' approach; innovative and creative concepts are needed. Of course, this cannot be implemented in a day or a year, at least not on a wide scale. Nevertheless, the concept should be clear, and any decision to establish part of the concept should be made in such a way that it does not compromise the total concept at a later stage.

Scales and responsibilities

The concept approach affects decisions on different scales. For instance, to create balanced material use, it is necessary to consider what affects material consumption the most. On the scale of a single building, the impact is limited. The decision to build has already been taken: a building cannot be built without materials, and the builder can only choose from the materials available on the market. A combination of measures and responsibilities on different scales, involving more, different, stakeholders, will have more impact. For example, the Government Building Agency in the Netherlands is responsible for numerous offices; though it does not build itself, it decides what and where to build. It has adopted a strategy which supports the balanced materials concept, which states: the first option is not to build (can the need for office space be met in another way?) The next option is to renovate an existing office or to extend it, and only if these two options are unavailable will new construction be considered. Essentially, the *Trias Ecologica* approach is being applied here at the planning level. Thus the concept is made up of elements that have to be implemented by different stakeholders and also applied, but at the planning level. It also shows another important lesson learned from the recent history of sustainable building development: the importance of organisation. Many options require a high level of organisation. Well-organised sustainable building management can provide more environmental benefit than technology, and at different levels: in policy development, in management, and in design.

The product chain is very important in the whole construction cycle: what products are on the market, how are they produced, what basic resources do they use, how can recycled materials be fed into this chain, what renewable alternatives are available or can be developed? It is here that major environmental benefits can be achieved, allowing architects to choose from environmentally-sound options in the design phase, once the decision to build has been taken.

The human cycle

The overall concept of sustainable housing is not just about environmental effects. However difficult, cultural and social elements also need to be incorporated. Managing resources is an environmental requirement, but sustainable development has a double target: to minimise the impact on the environment and to maximise the well-being of people. Any conceptual approach must be in line with the cultural and social values of the society that it is intended for, to make sure that people accept the developments, caring for the built environment and ensuring its longevity.

Socio-cultural analysis can be difficult, and developing a concrete built environment is often a matter of interpretation. Jaime Lerner, architect and former Mayor of Curitiba, Brazil, a city which is regarded as the most advanced in supporting sustainability on a human scale, gives us some clues when he refers to "the street as a synthesis of life", and says "The more mixed functions, the more human a city is". This rings true in many different cultures. In fact, it could be said that mono-functional design and planning expresses a linear (or one dimensional) approach, whereas mixing functions can be seen as a circular (or multi-dimensional) approach. We currently have the nascent understanding that the environmental elements of sustainability (i.e., physical ones) and the human ones support each other. The Dutch research programme Perspectives (which followed twelve families for two years while they tried to reduce their energy consumption) found that people considered more time-consuming and costly options more comfortable than the technological alternatives: for instance, dining out instead of cooking at

This personal mobile archieve allows flexible use of working space. This can have major influence on the amount of resources needed for office construction.

home, or a collective laundry system instead of doing their own washing (both of which can save energy and materials). These facilities can be brought together in a 'service concept' where functions and activities are provided as a service, instead of offering technology-based solutions. Compare this with the strategy of the Dutch Government Building Agency: if they can provide space as a service (by re-using empty buildings), or by offering tele-working spaces around the country, thereby avoiding the expense and congestion associated with travelling to a new centralised building, the need is met, and consumption of resources avoided. The 'service' concept has only just started to evolve, improving comfort and quality of life, preserving the built environment and eliminating rebound effects.

Economics

The concept approach to the economy requires special attention. On the one hand, some aspects of a sustainable concept may be more costly than others. This makes it difficult to implement sustainability, given current perceptions of economics and values. To overcome this, economies of scale can be implemented for some products (after initial support), or the developments can be directly supported through tax measures and subsidies (e.g., levies on environmental impacts, like a carbon tax, or tax rebates for efficient products). However, sustainable elements need not always be more expensive, and they may even be cheaper. In fact, most measures are, in the end, cheaper, and experience has shown that, based on a good concept, even the total cost of a housing project need not to be more expensive. When sustainability leads to clearly cheaper options, the implementation by the building stakeholders will become successful. On the other hand, this can lead to possible rebound effects, with owners or inhabitants spending the money they saved on other activities with a new environmental impact. (As mentioned, in the Netherlands garden lighting is becoming increasingly popular; and even air conditioners are sometimes installed.) A policy is required that gets people to invest in activities with a low environmental impact, thus bringing about a true lessening of pressure on the environment. Further research in this area is required.

Economics and the cost of sustainable building A nice example of how the market and costs can shift is illustrated by the introduction of high-efficiency glass in the Netherlands, (double glazing with a coating). When it was first introduced, this was more expensive than double glazing (though more energy-efficient), but none of the glass suppliers were interested in developing the market, or using their advertising budget promoting a more expensive option The Netherlands Agency for Energy and the Environment (Senter-Novem) arranged a meeting of all suppliers and proposed initiating a common campaign if the suppliers were willing to support this by up-scaling their production and providing information about high-efficiency glass in leaflets and on their websites. By acting together in this way, none of the suppliers would be profiting from another's investment, and the competition for consumers was eliminated as well. For the companies, it made no difference whether they sold regular double glazing or high-efficiency glass, as long as the change was made collectively. The proposal was agreed on, and within a few years high-efficiency glass took over the entire market at very competitive prices. Another example is softwood. Fifteen years ago softwood was twice as expensive as hardwood in the Netherlands. Now, after many market reforms, it costs the same, and with hardwood we have even seen a shift towards FSC wood from sustainable plantations. (Hardwood consumption per capita in the Netherlands is still among the highest in the world.) ■

The need for change towards innovative policies is shown by this poster campaign conducted by the Dutch government. It says: *'Can't the dikes be raised even more?'* And the pay-off line is *'different climate, different policy.'* The aim of the campaign is to prepare the Dutch for a different approach to land use and water management policies in response to climate and environmental changes.
Source: Ronald Rovers

Although it may seem contradictory, one lesson learned in the Netherlands is that to avoid these rebound effects, the elements of sustainable building do not necessarily need to be less expensive. Economic measures should be carefully designed and adapted to support and strengthen sustainable development, not only for short-term local gains but also to achieve overall long-term environmental benefits throughout the society. In fact, this could be seen as a general pre-condition for the development of sustainable building: if a measure does not support the shift towards sustainability, the economic system, which is a set of rules created to support our development, should be changed (even before attempting to change people's social and cultural behaviour).

Policies

The foregoing is, of course, closely related to policies, and the necessity of changing policies to support more sustainable solutions. Without effective policies and supporting measures, little will happen. If something is not mandatory, profitable or comfortable, the majority of people and stakeholders will not adopt it of their own accord. Experience has shown that initially, at least, many sustainable building concepts are difficult to get implemented; they may be a bit more expensive and require a change in practice and, of course, they are unknown. These are all elements which can be influenced by policy. Well-designed policies can be used to regulate the necessary areas of sustainable building.

Mindset
From linear to circular

Traditionally, materials are mined, buildings are constructed, basic maintenance is carried out, the building is heated with some easily available energy source, and after a while the building collapses, either of its own accord, or it is pulled down. In the past, this was less of a problem, since the demolished or collapsed building provided resources for a new building. This was easy: since no complicated methods were involved, bricks and wood elements were taken from the old building instead having to be collected from far away.

From linear to circulair: on different scales and by different stakeholders
Source: Ronald Rovers

Concepts(examples)	Stakeholders	From: Linear ('D')	Via: ('C') best practice	And: ('B') state-of-the-art	To: Circular
Materials level		fossil to waste	→	→	Renewables recycled
Building level		'Dust to Dust'	→	→	'Building to Building'
		Energy need	→	→	Energy producing
Neighbourhood		'Plug and play'	→	→	Eco-service zero emissions
			→	→	
Regional		'Use and dump'	→	→	'Urban harvesting'
		Demolish and renew	→	→	Stock recycling

Changing the context

To really make a shift towards a sustainably-built environment, it is not enough to work within the given political and economic frameworks. (Payback time is often used to judge investments, but this is only valid within the given political and economic context. If this context changes, the pay-back time changes and sustainable solutions become economical.)

This process can be illustrated with a conceptual approach studied a few years ago. The question was: how can we improve our environmental efficiency by a factor of 20 (i.e., with 5% of today's impact) while broadly maintaining our present welfare. Part of the research was aimed at building and housing. It turned out that this could only be achieved by focusing on existing housing stock, where an absolute reduction in environmental pressure can be achieved, but not with new construction. This involves establishing a conceptual framework (compare with the circular or 'A' situation described above) for the existing stock, to be in place in, say, 40 years. Since this would be impossible in the existing context, it was investigated how this context could be changed using the 'backcasting' method. The target (concept) for 2040 was defined and it was then determined what needs to be achieved in the period leading up to this date, going backwards in steps to define the necessary actions: looking back to see what is needed to make the action possible, and back again to define what conditions are required for the action to be possible, etc. The approach was then applied in a real situation, a neighbourhood in Rotterdam. In this way complete and coherent sets of measures and activities can be defined to reach that target, and change the context.

While forecasting leads to a diverse range of activities with varied effects, backcasting concentrates all actions on a targeted approach towards a well-defined concept for a future situation.

In this book, the DCBA method is used to illustrate the different phases that need to be established, going from daily practice, through small improvements, to best practice and state-of-the-art, or beyond. This is the route towards mid-term improvements, and higher targets have to be set each time. Backcasting, however, uses similar targets, but they are derived from an integrated view of a desired future situation. For longer-term policies, this provides a much better guarantee that policies are mutually supportive and will work towards implementing concepts that can cover more aspects (up to the whole built environment). The steps that are required can be defined by tracking back what has to be done to achieve the integrated solution, at various levels and for all stakeholders. In addition, this clarifies how the policy, social, institutional and economic contexts could (or should) change as part of the desired route towards a sustainable built environment.

It is estimated that a 'B' target level can be achieved in the Netherlands through incremental changes (i.e., without changing institutional or main financial arrangements). Further improvements (on a national scale) would be possible too, but would require various contextual changes (e.g. in organisational and financial arrangements). ∎

lessons learned

This chapter has given a general overview of sustainable housing and the issues associated with it. The construction of a new housing project must be seen in the context of the totality of human activities and structures. When a new housing project is decided upon, this has to be done in the context of existing policies and economic structures, based on people's wishes and everyday building practice. The rest of this book describes how we deal with this in the Netherlands, and the lessons we have learned.

Some lessons:
* Concepts instead of measures
* Global systems, but local resources
* Process innovation, before technology innovation
* Start from overall stock management, not from focus on new buildings
* Economic system has to be adapted
* In the end: legislation & regulation necessary
* Use demonstration projects
* Do not copy other culture/climate examples ∎

However, ninety-five percent of today's buildings were constructed after the industrial revolution and are not well suited for re-use. At best, old cement can be ground up and used as gravel for other building projects. Continuing to think in a linear fashion, with a one time use of resources (for ever shorter periods of time), will ultimately lead to the disappearance of cultures, as occurred on a small scale on Easter Island and with the Mayan culture.

The main priority we have to address is, therefore, the mindset required to create a sustainable approach to the built environment: to bring about a change from linear to circular thinking. This needs to take place in the design, planning and management of the built environment, at all levels, from technology development and stock maintenance, to housing and economic policy, supported by system changes across the boundaries and concepts described above.

Ambition

Brandevoort:
Traditional architecture
at one of the best
received projects
in the Netherlands:
apparently it comes
close to people's
cultural and social
perceptions of housing.
Source: Ronald Rovers

Of course, the whole process of change takes time. Different goals need to be set in different situations and at different stages of development. Any specific concepts and measures, however, must be selected in such a way that they do not prevent the total concept and overall goal being realised at a later stage.

DCBA method

The *DCBA method* is a classification model for all kinds of sustainable building measures. Materials, ideas and measures are classified in four levels:

D : The normal situation
C : Correct normal use
B : Minimize impact
A : Autonomy, the most favourable situation

This method can be used throughout the building process, in all stages. For example, it can serve as a discussion tool for various stakeholders in the early stages of the project, or after completion it can be used to evaluate whether the design has achieved its objectives .

The *DCBA method* was developed by BOOM for the demonstration project Ecolonia, Alphen a/d Rijn in 1993.

In this book, we generally analyse ambitions and clarify targets using a DCBA structure, which defines the goals at different levels: from business as usual (D), via better (C), to good (B), and most wanted (A). This has proven a very useful and practical instrument, and shows that there can be steps in moving from the linear to a circular process.

Policies: transforming the market

One demonstration project does not bring about a nationwide switch to sustainable building practices, but it has proven to be an important element in an overall government sustainable building strategy. Creating an overall strategy, however, requires the development of a balanced, integrated approach, that allows for gradual change towards greater sustainability, by simultaneously improving various aspects of sustainable building (as described in other chapters) and several present-day quality standards. This policy process is referred to as the 'market transformation strategy' and integrates concepts and tools to describe and demonstrate ways to initiate an effective building market transformation. Demonstration projects have proven to be a crucial factor in this policy process, as 'seeing is believing' in the building and construction sectors.

Today's policies are based on developments in the 1970s and 1980s, when societies suddenly became aware of their dependence on limited natural resources, like energy and minerals (inspired by the 1973 oil crisis, Club of Rome report, etc). Later on, resources like clean air and water became important too. The initial policies targeted so-called 'end-of-pipe' measures: sealing leaks in homes, for example, and adding insulation to roofs. These policies were supported by government information campaigns to home owners, and by subsidies for specific energy-saving measures.

Later on, typically in the 1990s, the concept of an integrated approach took hold, and the policy focus moved from stopping 'leaks' to preventing these from being created in the first place. Thus, new combinations of policies were designed that require a minimum energy performance level for new buildings, but which also promote the implementation of more advanced techniques and designs. In addition,

Policy Route

Sustainable building can be directed through policy. Initially, policies will focus on stimulating certain beneficial building practices (e.g. techniques, designs), and preventing the use of unfavourable options. Over the years, policies in the Netherlands, as in most European countries, have been integrated into balanced frameworks. These policies set minimum standards for various aspects of buildings (e.g., minimum levels of cavity wall insulation; maximum levels for radon emissions in houses), but for some aspects (mainly energy consumption) these standards also define a minimum overall performance that has to be met when building houses or other buildings. In the Netherlands, several policies have been implemented over the years to increase the performance of buildings. The best developed policy area is building energy consumption, which has a tradition of more than 20 years in Dutch policy-making. The policies pursued to regulate energy consumption have evolved over the years, as have the energy efficiency levels to be achieved in new buildings.

The continuous increase in energy efficiency has been steered by a combination of policies:
• Minimum energy performance standards, which set a threshold which has to be met when a new building is constructed;
• Negotiated agreements, specific local rules and subsidies to stimulate higher energy performance levels for new buildings;
• Research & development, demonstration and market introduction projects to create even better performing energy-options and to introduce these into the market.
The policies are regularly reviewed and the required performance levels adapted (for each type of policy) in response to improvements made on the market. Over the years this produces a steadily improving building stock, with new buildings being more energy-efficient than in previous years. This policy process can be described as a 'market transformation' strategy: a widely applied strategy to increase the energy performance of products. ■

it was realised that electricity consumption was quickly increasing, and policies where implemented to promote CFLs (Compact Fluorescent Lights). In the late 1990s, an energy tax was introduced (for households and small businesses) to to create a strong driver for energy conservation. Unfortunately, this tax proved not to be very successful, as the consumer response was driven a lot less by cost concerns than had been assumed. Part of the tax, however, was reserved for rebates (for home insulation, efficient appliances, and small-scale renewable energy systems). Especially in the area of appliances, these rebates have created a significant market transformation.

During the 1990s, it was realised that sustainable building policies should cover more than building energy consumption, and efforts are now being made to raise other building-related policies (e.g., materials consumption) to the same level as energy. Current thinking is that governments should also focus on a long-term transition to sustainable practices (in building, energy supply, etc).

Strong public policies required

Transforming the built environment to create a more sustainable situation is a very demanding task. Buildings have many different aspects which often need to be improved simultaneously, while the building sector is highly diversified and has to meet a lot of competing demands. Creating new buildings which are healthy to live in and well-insulated, provide adequate comfort but do not overuse scarce resources, are designed to last a lifetime but at a minimum first cost, is too demanding for a sole project developer, architect or contractor.

Experience has shown that benefits from more sustainable designs are often accumulated over many years, but the initial cost has to be paid in advance. Many more sustainable design options must be developed, but these will only be cost-effective if there is a large-scale market, creating a learning curve and adequate turnover to justify the investment in product development. Another complicating factor is that benefits are often social or societal benefits (e.g., better living conditions, reduced impact on the environment), whilst the costs are borne by the individual having the building constructed. This calls for adequate government policies which take into account the current situation, but shift it towards a more sustainable situation over time.

Market transformation strategy

A standard framework for this kind of government policy is the market transformation strategy. This strategy was developed internationally in the 1980s and 1990s, mainly as a means to create a change in the market for appliances (towards greater energy-efficiency). Although not many countries have formally adopted a market transformation strategy for buildings, most have implemented several policies that – together – work to move the market in the direction of better-performance buildings, exactly as the strategy describes.

Market transformation rests on a combination of requirements. The first requirement for an effective policy is to have standard measurement procedures to determine the quality of a building or an aspect of a building. A measurement procedure (also known as test standard) can be very simple (e.g., a measure of insulation thickness), or very complicated (e.g., a calculation of the total environmental impact of the building materials used). Without standard measurements, it is impossible to compare building designs or buildings and thus impossible to apply a strategy to promote better buildings or preferred products.

The second requirement is to classify the performance of products, building designs or buildings, in terms of all aspects deemed relevant to sustainable building. Experience has shown that it is preferable to classify the performance of buildings according to performance levels. Performance classifications can be based on efficiency (e.g., maximum heating energy demand per square metre, minimum noise reduction of a wall), or on absolute performance (e.g., maximum indoor air pollution level). The classification should include current practices (ranging from very poor to very good), as well as the optimum condition.

Based on these two requirements, performance levels can be determined. Ideally, three levels can be set:
• A minimum performance level, which has to be met by all buildings.
• A best practice level, which describes the level that can reasonably be achieved with a good design and with good building practice.
• A state-of-the-art level, which describes the maximum level that could be achieved in the current context.

The first, minimum performance level is laid down by law, and official enforcement is crucial at this level. The second, best practice level is often used for official government endorsement purposes (e.g. subsidies, government procurement policies), to stimulate the market but which does not have to be enforced by law. The third, state-of-the-art level is usually set by government as a target for the future. It is used to promote and demonstrate new options, thus making these more acceptable in daily practice. This strategy has so far proven to be successful in reducing heating energy demand for new houses, and in product energy consumption.

The market transformation strategy works with a combination of policies to ban the worst building designs from the market, raise awareness of sustainable building issues, educate professionals (and sometimes the public) about the options for improving buildings and to prove the viability of new designs in demonstration projects or design competitions. Ultimately, the strategy builds on the ability to move to constantly higher sustainable building quality levels (which is enabled by the strategy itself): what is the best practice one year, could well be the minimum performance level a few years later, etc.

A special element in the market transformation strategy is communication with market parties about the classification. For appliances, there are 7-class energy labels in Europe, which show the relative performance of the product compared to others. A similar label is currently being implemented in a number of European countries for existing homes, but it is still too early to know whether it will be effective. It should be considered, however, that in building market transformation the actual 'customers' are often not the home occupants but the project developer, designer and/or builder, and it may be more effective to target policies at these parties.

Of course, building policy does not operate in a vacuum. Architects and contractors can only apply better products, materials, technologies and design options if these are available to them. Thus, there is a strong link with product policy, promoting products that are less polluting and consume less energy during production, which are made from renewable resources (or at least from resources with less environmental impact), and offer improved design and functionality.

Building market transformation policies
Source:
Frank Klinckenberg

The graph shows the relationship between the performance of buildings (or building designs) and the policies that are applied to improve this performance. The graph is based on the changes in energy performance commonly seen in products (appliances, heating installations, etc.). It is believed, however, that a similar situation will apply to numerous aspects of sustainable building as well.

Product policies can regulate the characteristics of a product (health, safety, energy consumption, etc.) or subsidies can be used to endorse specific products, but the embedded product characteristics can also be influenced by industry policy (e.g. levies on scarce resources, production waste, industrial energy consumption; carbon emission reduction schemes). For example, a building materials industry, like a cement factory, in the Netherlands has

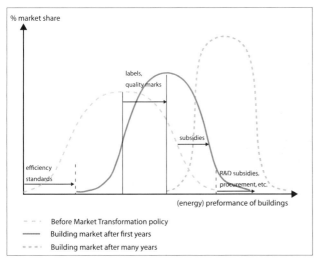

- - - Before Market Transformation policy
───── Building market after first years
- - - Building market after many years

to comply with energy targets (per unit of production), emission targets, and has to obtain water and resource extraction permits, which are conditional on the balance that the company will create between the damage to the environment created by these extractions and the effort made to compensate for this by creating 'new nature'.

At national level, building policies relate to national sustainable development policies, but are also linked to the general economic policies of a country. Naturally, building policies must deliver their share of national energy efficiency and (non-renewable) resource consumption targets, and to the reduction of carbon emissions. However, building policies also have to deal with the economic development of a country: as people get wealthier, they generally want larger and more comfortable homes. As the environmental impact of buildings is closely linked to their size, this trend puts additional pressure on the need to decouple economic development and environmental performance. Policies in the Netherlands include, for example, a ban on new housing developments outside of current town limits (to prevent urban sprawl), and a calculation of the energy demand of new-built areas. This field may be extended in future policies, e.g. by promoting the re-use of materials or of entire constructions, or by limiting the energy and water demand of a housing area, independent of the size of the house.

Building policies also relate to social policies. Adequate housing, for example, is considered to be a social entitlement. People also have a social (or cultural) bond with their built environment, and many people do not welcome large scale demolition of housing blocks to make way for new developments, or the relocation of communities. Consideration of these issues is seen as a public right too, and should be taken into account when building policies are developed.

The Dutch pavilion at the Hanover World Expo (2000), designed by MVRDV, demonstrates trends in sustainable building: on land use (multi-level functions), compactness, integration of renewable energy (5th floor), preserving greenery (3rd floor), and reducing environmental impact, within a natural setting. An option for the future?
Source: Juan Ayala

Dutch building policies

Energy consumption is the best-developed aspect of Dutch building policies; many other aspects were added later to the regulatory framework..The actual framework is described under 'regulations'. A brief description of best practice and the state-of-the-art standards is included here to demonstrate the practical application of this strategy.

The Dutch government has set minimum energy performance standards for energy and some other aspects, and many best practice standards for energy, materials and water consumption. There are a variety of standards for materials with reduced environmental impacts which have sometimes been supported with subsidies, and sometimes endorsed in government communications. Additionally, many local governments require new buildings to meet certain best practice standards, or endorse this. State-of-the-art standards have seldom been set in the Netherlands; support (mainly in the form of R&D grants or subsidies) has been widely available for many advanced techniques. This has seldom been formally linked to other policies, however, and many new techniques are making little progress in the building market. This is not necessarily caused by the low level of integration of policy, but better coordinated policies help to overcome these barriers.

Time line for transition

Transition of the building market from today's common practice to sustainability will take time. Small improvements often require a lot of effort on the part of building professionals, who need to master new techniques or new building practices, develop cost-effective ways of implementing improvements and find ways to pass on additional costs to the occupants of a new building.

Radical improvements in buildings may require new concepts in resource consumption and living standards (see chapter on concepts), as well as breakthrough technical solutions. These changes need to be developed in cooperation with others, and tested and demonstrated in real-life situations, so that they are available when societies are ready to adopt them, or when external pressure (e.g., energy supply issues) demand radical changes. Government R&D support appears to be the only way to speed up this trend, as only governments can afford to invest in long-term, often complex, technological opportunities.

The most important aspect of a policy, however, is time: it may be impossible to improve the quality of buildings overnight, but it is certainly achievable to do so over a number of years. It is essential to have an integrated strategy, and to gradually raise performance standards over the course of time.

Legislation and Standards

In previous decades central and local government used many different instruments to promote and try to implement greater sustainability in the building sector. Various methods have been applied: subsidies, tax measures, voluntary agreements, demonstration projects, market campaigns, investment schemes, labelling schemes, assessment tools and more. Although these tools have to some extent been successful and still play an important part in helping to create a more sustainable built environment, experience has shown that the energy consumption and environmental performance of dwellings and non-residential buildings need to be anchored in legislation and standards.

There are several reasons for this:

- First and foremost, experience has shown that only the frontrunners take up the newest insights and technologies in sustainable building. To get the full market to improve environmental performance and sustainability, legislation and standards have proven to be a necessity.
- Secondly, regulation is necessary to prevent too great a diversity between regions or countries. Architects and contractors do not want to have to deal with different requirements and approaches for every project and in each new place (especially in a small country like the Netherlands where companies work nationally).
- Thirdly, legislation sets a minimum standard which can be achieved by most. It always guarantees a certain minimum level, which then can still be surpassed.

CASE STUDY

Backcasting as a tool for policy design

Policy design for sustainable development can be a tailored process to maximise impact in a local situation. The Dutch Sustainable Technology Development programme (STD) applied the backcasting method to sustainable housing development in a Rotterdam neighbourhood to identify the technological and policy changes that would be required to achieve a dramatic reduction in the environmental impact of building and housing. The environmental challenges (in terms of energy & materials demand, the water cycle, pollution, traffic, liveability, etc.) were analysed, along with technological and organisational solutions to improve the situation in the neighbourhood. It was shown that some solutions would only be feasible in the (near) future, either because more technical development was needed, or because they depended on other measures being implemented first. For example, the water management in the area could be improved, but only if the traffic situation was first improved to release land that is now being used for roads and parking. The analysis resulted in a long-term agenda for sustainable housing development in the area, identifying short, medium and long-term measures to be taken in the relevant areas. This agenda served as the basis for a short-term local government policy plan and provided much-needed inspiration for medium and long-term policies at national level. ∎

Some history

It all began with energy. The energy legislation route took about 20 years. Setting the regulations for other environmental aspects is now taking the same route with one exception: noise reduction or, more broadly, acoustic quality. The Noise Pollution Act, which deals with pollution between houses and between traffic and buildings (see chapter 2 Comfort and Climate), was already in place by the early 1980s. A development always starts with a formal document from a government department. Even now for energy and the environment, either the minister of housing or the minister of economic affairs still formulate many official documents which set out the vision and the policy outlines for the coming years. Sometimes such a document or an official letter to parliament is drafted in such a way that it will elicit comments from the wider public. Over the past decade the Dutch ministry of the environment has produced five documents on its National Environmental Policy Strategy. Other important publications included 'Implementing Environment Policy', 'Action programme on Health and the Environment', 'Environmental Policy Document', 'Second policy document on People, Aims and Quality of Life: Environmental Policy 2002- 2006,' etc.

If a policy strategy is agreed by parliament the requirements are incorporated in building regulations or environmental codes. These regulations and codes lay down the standards which must be met to show that a building or construction meets the set performance standards. To start building a building permit is required. In order to obtain this permit, the project has to be demonstrated with drawings and

PERFORMANCE CONCEPT

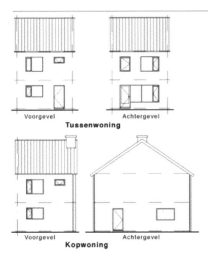

Voorgevel   Achtergevel
Tussenwoning

Voorgevel   Achtergevel
Kopwoning

Dutch Reference House (1-family house)
Source: SenterNovem

Variation on the same theme: modern version of the reference house (Zoetermeer) *Source: SenterNovem*

calculations (using the standards prescribed in the building regulations) that the building meets all the performance requirements.

Overview of political measures
Energy performance building standards

Around 1960, some vague recommendations on saving energy were made. Slowly a transformation took place, gradually moving from separate, recommended measures and recommendations to mandatory packages of measures, until today, with performance requirements for whole buildings. The first was the Model Building Ordinance, a code adopted partly or in full by municipalities. Each municipality was free to apply the model as they saw fit. This bylaw laid down the requirements to be met for building materials (in terms of thickness, insulation values, etc). From 1975 on, a great deal was invested in energy-saving measures in the Netherlands. Up until 1995 municipalities could set their own requirements for the energy performance of a building based on their local model building ordinance or bylaw.

During the 1990s, National Packages were introduced for dwellings. These included a coherent set of measures which could be used individually or in combination. The use of these measures provided credit points which, based on an agreement with the financial sector, could provide access to better financing schemes (e.g., lower mortgage interest rates). After 1995 the legislation and standardisation increased dramatically. It was realised that rules should not simply dictate requirements for materials, but prescribe the desired performance. It should be left to the market parties to decide how to fill in these requirements or meet these performance standards.

Energy performance coefficient (EPC)

In 1995, the National Building Regulations were introduced, which set the performance requirements for the whole building. This performance requirement is expressed as an Energy Performance Coefficient (EPC). In 1995, the EPC for dwellings was 1.4, which at the time represented an improvement of about 10% in energy use. The method for calculating the EPC is laid down in the Dutch standards: NEN 5128 (dwellings) and NEN 2916 (non-residential buildings). (An English version of these standards is available.) It took about ten years to develop them. These standards have been revised a few times (further to new techniques) and the required performance level has also been changed twice in the building regulations. In 1998 the EPC changed to 1.2 and in 2000 to 1.0. In 2006 the EPC was lowered again, this time to 0.8, and a reduction to 0.6 is foreseen in 2011.

Energy performance of the location (EPL)

Based on the growing understanding that an integrated approach is required to improve the energy performance of a building, it became clear that many energy-efficiency measures needed to be applied at the neighbourhood level, because many technical installations are more efficient when they deal with larger volumes. For this reason an energy indicator for a site or whole location was developed and introduced. Besides the mandatory EPC, the government developed the EPL (Energy Performance Location indicator) which, for the time being, is a voluntary performance indicator. This EPL means that energy aspects can be introduced which are outside the scope of the house building and construction sectors, but which have a positive impact on the energy consumption of a building (e.g. energy-efficient heat and electricity generation, collective facilities, heat delivery, etc.). Usually it is the municipality that sets a target for EPL to support the improved performance of individual buildings.

Covenants
In the past (1998-2002) the government tried to conclude voluntary agreements with housing associations. The aim was to implement energy saving measures in their housing to provide a better energy performance standard for the building than the minimum performance laid down in the building regulations, but these agreements have not been successful.

Existing residential buildings and dwellings
In fact, all existing housing must meet the basic requirements of the building regulations for dwellings. The regulations lay down certain rules on ventilation related to health and energy consumption. In the Netherlands there is a tool which can be used to quantify the energy consumption of existing buildings: the EPA (Energy Performance Assessment). Using a computer model an expert can make recommendations on how to improve the construction and installations of a building to reduce its energy consumption. This is a voluntary scheme.

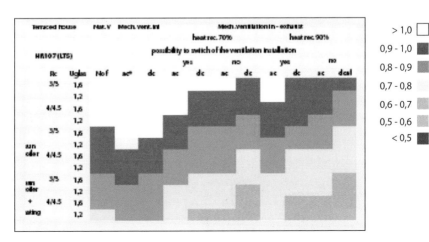

The figure shows how to meet the required Energy Performance level through different combinations of climate control installations and insulation values of the building. In order to meet future performance standards (was 1.0; now 0.8), it is clear that this can only be met by including heat recovery from ventilation air. Only one option without is available (natural ventilation), with very high insulation levels (bottom left corner).
Source: SenterNovem

EU Energy Performance Directive (EPBD)

The EU has recently enacted legislation on energy conservation. This stipulates that each country has to have minimum requirements for the energy consumption of buildings. Existing buildings must have a label for the energy efficiency of the building. Heating and ventilation installations must be regularly checked. These standards were developed by CEN (the European Standardisation Organisation). As of 1 January 2008, all buildings in the Netherlands, including existing ones, will require an energy label similar to that currently on all electrical appliances.

Traffic performance indicator on location (TPF)

Parallel to the energy performance of a location, a traffic performance indicator for a location has also been developed, known as TPF. (There is also an English version available.) This tool provides guidance on how to plan and design part of or even a whole town in such a way that transport connections are efficient and that energy consumption by traffic is reduced as much as possible.

Energy and legislation goals

The energy consumption of a newly-built dwelling decreased from 3000 m³ gas to 800 m³, but this was offset by an increase in electricity consumption, caused mainly by household appliances. Step-by-step new building directives, standards and guidelines are being set up to establish new minimum standards. But these are still minimum levels and, for the time being, only for new buildings. A whole new set of standards and regulations is needed to steer the building sector towards a real shift and an absolute reduction in resource consumption and environmental impacts. The target for the coming decades is to build homes which are affordable, energy neutral (no use of fossil fuels), made of renewable and recycled materials, with local management of water, in inspiring and people-oriented neighbourhoods.

'De Goede Woning' in Lobith
Source: SenterNovem

The environment and legislation

The first legislation clearly focusing on environmental issues was the act that limited the use of asbestos in building materials. It was during a period when there was a growing belief and concern that production and consumption should change and become more controlled. Prompted by events like Rio '92 and the Kyoto Agreement, a whole set of rules and regulations was introduced on production emissions, product performance during use and disposal – all intended to avoid damage to the environment. At the same time, regulations were introduced to clean up already polluted areas, like rivers and soil. The health aspect is currently seen as more important, partly as a result of incorrectly insulated buildings (built too airtight or with poor or incorrect ventilation and/or heating installations) A key concept in modern environmental policy is total chain management. It is a technique that involves assessing and managing the environmental effects of products throughout their lifecycle, from extraction of raw materials through to the disposal of waste. To make total chain management work in practice information is needed about the overall environmental impact of a product. Various tools have been developed to assess such information. These include the Life Cycle Analyses (LCA) and the eco-indicator.

Materials performance building standards

Some years ago a project was instigated to set up standards and legislation to qualify the environmental impact of a building (in Dutch MMG). A draft standard was developed but not followed up with regulations and a performance definition. The stakeholders (contractors and manufacturers) were concerned about the complexity of the method and passed a "vote of no confidence" on the data used for materials and products. The government recently decided not to implement this standard in legislation. New avenues are being sought to deal with this issue.

Standard for radon radiation

The radon radiation standard was set up from a health and safety point of view. The standard has been completed but has not been implemented in legislation also because of opposition from the building industry.

Subsidies in the Netherlands
(2005)
Source: Piet Heijnen

	Netherlands: what is subsidized?	At which stage and how?
VAMIL	production of energy from biomass	tax instrument, investor can write off at any moment lowering fiscal profit: liquidity advantage
EIA, MIA	investment in renewables	tax instrument, Part of investment lowers fiscal profit
'Green loan'	financing of "green projects"	a) green investment fond: Lower financial return is balanced by tax office. b) lower mortgages for financing projects
REB	stimulate buying "green" (this year replaced by..)	tax on products, lower electricity tariffs for "green" electricity
MEP	stimulate the production of "green" electricity	fixed subsidy per produced KWh (guaranteed for 10 years)
EOS - LT	Subsidies long term fundamental research	Subsidies 100% fundamental resarch of energy related items
EOS - Demo	Subsidies demonstration projects	Subsidies 40% of the more investments of innovative items, compared with a reference situation
NEO	Subsidies short term research	Broad playing field for new developments
UKR	Subsidies items concerning energy transition	...
IS	Subsidies innovative cooperation between different parties	Concerns production or development of sustainable products or processes

Tools development

The LCA (*Life Cycle Analysis*) is an internationally accepted method for accurately identifying and assessing the environmental impact that occurs in all phases of the lifecycle of a product, process, service or material. The method produces an 'environmental profile' that shows how the product scores 'from cradle to grave' in relation to up to 14 environmental effects. The LCA underpins many, for the moment voluntary, tools used to compare buildings and product performances.

Eco-indicator

An eco-indicator reduces the results of an LCA to a single figure. This figure expresses the environmental impact caused by a product or material 'from cradle to grave'. Ecoquantum, Greencalc and Dubocalc are three well-known computer programs used to calculate the eco-indicator.

MRPI

Further to LCAs and the eco-indicator, the building industry developed a system known as MRPI (*Milieu Relevante Product Informatie*: Environmentally- Relevant Product Information). This system provides standardised and validated information about the environmental impact of building materials. MRPI enables suppliers in the building industry to provide other parties in the industry with reliable and comparable environmental information about their products.

Waste legislation

For a long time the Netherlands was a frontrunner in the legislation and regulation of environmental matters. As part of a package of mandatory measures the

Standardisation process in the Netherlands

The formal standards office in the Netherlands is NEN, the Netherlands Standardisation Institute. This institute is a non-governmental organisation supported with public and private sector funding. The task of the institute is to facilitate Dutch standards committees and to ensure that the remit of each committee correctly reflects the work area.

At present about 150 people (NEN employees only) are involved in the work of standardisation. In the field of energy conservation, NEN set up a steering committee to coordinate all activities concerning energy standardisation. The standardisation work is carried out by various committees and subcommittees of which there are currently about 16, concerned only with energy-related matters. There are two committees working

in the area of Energy Performance Conservation. In the past these two committees set the standards for calculating the Energy Performance Coefficient (EPC) referred to the Dutch Building Regulations. All new buildings must meet this value to obtain a building permit and everyone has to use these standards to calculate this figure. Each committee or subcommittee is responsible for setting up a standard. It is therefore important for

all the relevant parties to be involved in a standards committee to defend their own interests. This means that a standard is always a compromise and not a maximum performance.

After a draft standard has been produced, the job of NEN is to ensure that all the relevant parties in the Netherlands have the opportunity to comment on the draft standards during a period of six months. After that period the

committee must respond to all the comments made and a final document is drawn up. NEN oversees that all the comments are properly dealt with and that there are no longer any fundamental objections. Some standards have become part of the building regulations, but most are used in building specifications and in private agreements between principals and contractors. ■

government introduced the Building Materials Decree (*Bouwstoffenbesluit*). This means that manufacturers are obliged to provide relevant environmental information on their products and materials. A label can be awarded on the basis of this decree.

The EU has a similar directive: the Construction Product Directive (1993) which deals with the quality of products, based on standards and procedures. Building products must meet certain fundamental requirements concerning hygiene, health and the environment, etc. The directive states that people must not be exposed to radiation or the risk of inhaling dangerous particles. By 2005 there were just a few EU measures for building products related to the environment. However introduction has accelerated and many tools based on the LCA are now available.

At the other end of the building process there has been legislation in place in the Netherlands since 1995 which bans the dumping of waste products. Precise rules are given on how to deal with building and other waste products. One of the successes of this legislation is that about 90% of building waste is now recycled.

The environment and aspirations

It is technically and theoretically feasible to quantify environmental effects but in practice, there is a still lot of debate surrounding these issues. The discussion concerns how to weigh the effect and importance of different items (e.g. water compared with green) and how sound is all the data? For the time being the debate will continue in both the Netherlands and in international fora. A standardised database for environmental figures is being set up in the Netherlands based on

Legislation in the Netherlands
Source: Piet Heijnen

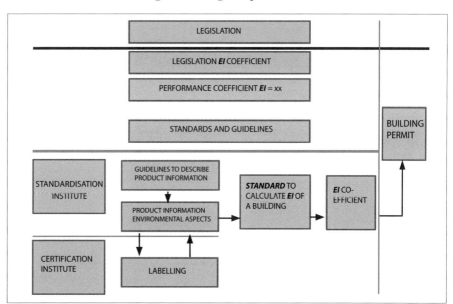

an agreement about weighing methods: how to weigh the selected environmental parameters with the tools Ecoquantum and Greencalc. The ultimate goal is to realise buildings which cause no environmental damage. The problem is how to integrate this into the framework of legal rules and standards. That is the task for the years to come.

2 Comfort and Climate

The Netherlands is located by the sea and has a mild, temperate climate. The weather conditions, however, can change very quickly depending on the wind direction. Apart from the natural climate, the environmental conditions also depend on human activities and buildings. Probably because of its high population density, this receives a lot of attention in the Netherlands. The basic conditions for what is considered a healthy and comfortable climate are laid down in standards. These standards concern thermal and hygric climate, acoustics and noise, natural light, air quality, wind speeds, and even odours, for both indoor and outdoor situations.

For the outdoors, for instance, to prevent nuisance in residential areas the Netherlands has designated 'silent areas' in different parts in the country. Noise zones and recently, odour zones have also been defined around certain, mainly industrial, areas with set maximum levels for noise or odours. These are important planning issues in the Netherlands. But even on a smaller scale, there is significant interaction between building design and outdoor conditions, for example, the high wind speeds that occur in high-rise urban areas. The same wind can also cause increased heat losses from façades.

Indoor conditions are generally well under control these days, to the extent that indoor air quality is sometimes better than outdoor quality. Materials and their long-term effects on health have been documented and regulated. Nevertheless in the Netherlands too, people's comfort demands have tended to increase and improving comfort is sometimes even used as a sales argument for energy-efficient technologies, such as low temperature heating systems or floor heating systems.

> Indoor comfort

Thermal comfort

The more comfortable and healthier buildings that are common today provide a starting point for the development of buildings in the future. This is a part of the sustainable development of the built environment. Higher standards for comfort and health in modern buildings could lead to more energy consumption. Thus, minimising energy and material use while improving health and comfort can be seen as an extra challenge. A realistic view of the future is one which anticipates the future needs of inhabitants. There are generally accepted conditions for comfort and health that will not change dramatically in future. Nevertheless, improvements now sometimes considered a luxury might well be standard in the future.

Thermal comfort in the cold season
Short history
Most dwellings in the Netherlands were fitted with central heating systems in the 1960s; these replaced local heating with coal or gas-fired stoves. The most commonly used system has radiators under the windows to avoid draughts and asymmetric radiant temperatures. This is a tankless system where the water is directly heated with natural gas, and the temperature is centrally controlled by a thermostat in the living room. Apart from individual heating systems, a boiler for a whole block or apartment building, known as a district heating system, is also used. District heating systems, which use the waste heat of electricity plants, have a long tradition in the Netherlands.

Typical design temperatures were 20°C (68°F) in living rooms and 18°C (64.4°F) in bedrooms, with 50-70°C (122°F-158°F) or higher for the radiators. This gradually changed to 21°C(69.8°F) throughout the dwelling, allowing the use of the space in the house to be changed without changing the heating system (flexibility). Nighttime setback was common. In apartment buildings there was often a single control for a whole block. This caused complaints, as well as unnecessarily high energy consumption.

Present situation
The required values for the physical parameters (air temperature, radiant temperature, air velocity, relative humidity, draughts, floor temperature, radiation asymmetry, vertical temperature gradient) are well-known. Any well-controlled heating system in dwellings built according to today's standards can meet these requirements. The overall efficiency of the heating system is much improved by the use of thermostats mounted on the radiators, a programmable central thermostat and a high-efficiency tankless system. Problems sometimes arise with poorly-designed air heating systems (air velocity, draughts and vertical temperature gradient), inadequate solar control (overheating by solar radiation) and when residents fail to take sufficient control over their thermal environment.

The radiator system is still the most common and the cheapest system, but air and floor heating systems are installed as well, mostly as part of an integrated approach which includes installation concepts (e.g. heat pumps, aquifers, etc.). See chapter 3 for examples of these installation concepts.

Future improvements
In well-insulated air-tight dwellings with insulating glazing, there will be hardly any problems with draughts and cold surfaces. If floors are covered with tiles, a floor heating system offers a very comfortable solution (sometimes combined with a radiator or a hot air convection system). A convection system may be selected mainly for its integration potential, with ventilation and promising ventilation heat re-use, but not for better thermal comfort. If rooms

are used intermittently a fast-reacting air heating system may be more energy saving. Further improvements in comfort can be expected from: lower air temperature and higher radiant temperature; a thermal climate that can be controlled by the resident according to the activity, with no uniform temperature in the whole house. In open spaces this can only be accomplished with heat radiation; better control of the solar energy entering through the windows.

Wall heating systems have been applied successfully to achieve a larger radiant component. Compared with a floor heating system the view factor to residents is larger resulting in a larger radiant component and avoiding too warm feet. However, obstructing objects such as cupboards are a problem. The use of enlarged radiators with a lower mean temperature is important only for the use of low temperature energy sources, such as solar heat and heat pumps. Low temperature systems are an important research area as they are expected to be the common systems in the far future. A problem of low energy buildings is that during the heating season, especially in autumn and spring, solar radiation can heat a room to uncomfortably high temperatures while it is still cold outside. Cooling with outside air or using a shading device, however, is a waste of energy. A faster reacting heating system (perhaps with an anticipating control) and more thermal mass (maybe phase change storage) could improve comfort without extra energy loss.

Thermal comfort in the warm season
Present situation
In the Netherlands the use of a cooling system in the warm season is not common and should not be necessary as there are only few days a year with temperatures above 30°C (86°F) and the mean daily temperature never reaches that value. Yet cooling units are sold for dwellings for people to create a more comfortable indoor climate in summer. There are several reasons for this. The units and the energy are relatively cheap for the prosperous inhabitants, the average age of the population is increasing, the comfort demands are higher and many well-insulated dwellings are very warm in summer. Overheating in summer can be solved by devoting more attention to the conceptual design of a dwelling (e.g., solar control, shading, summer ventilation).

The required values for the physical parameters (i.e., air temperature, radiant temperature, air velocity) in the warm season are less clear than the values for the cold season. There are indications that in a warm climate higher indoor temperatures are acceptable than in a mild climate. An indoor temperature that is much lower than the outdoor temperature can cause a heat shock. The maximum acceptable values for air humidity are, above all, determined by the risk of mould growth and not by the resident's comfort. For a person at rest humidity is not very important. Humidity (i.e., skin wetness) only becomes an important comfort parameter at increased levels of activity.

Risks and choices

A sustainable design in terms of Life Cycle Analysis (LCA) and energy use, will not automatically result in a comfortable and healthy design. Comfort issues like asymmetric radiation indoors, cold floors and draughts are problems which can be solved, but there are other risks which need special attention.

Thermal comfort issues:

- Overheating: solar gains and internal gains combined can create a high temperature due to high insulation levels. Uncomfortably high temperatures (overheating) are easily reached even in the heating season.
- Too high humidity: when ventilation is kept to the minimum level necessary for air quality, vapour production inside the house can lead to extreme air humidity. This in turn could be the cause of allergens in the air (e.g., moulds and mites). Special attention must be paid to ventilation in the kitchen and bathroom to total ventilation if laundry is dried indoors or if there are many houseplants.
- Thermal bridges have a higher relative surface humidity (i.e., increased risk of moulds) than in a non-insulated house. As a result of insulation, the exterior side of the insulated wall is colder which enhances the thermal bridge effect.
- In the heating season interstitial condensation is more likely to occur on the cold side of the insulation. More attention must be paid to vapour barriers in walls and roof. In summer, interstitial condensation (summer condensation) could occur in the interior part of the insulation, especially when the house is cooled.
- Entrapped moisture in envelopes (e.g., through the use of wet insulation material during the construction) can cause serious moisture problems.
- Air flow through the insulation can also cause condensation and must be avoided.
- Reducing window size in order to reduce overheating problems and less heat loss can result in more use of artificial light. If the focus is on daylight there is a risk of overheating and more energy losses.

Passive versus Active

Installations:
There is sometimes a debate about the choice between passive and active measures, as in the case of natural ventilation or forced ventilation. It has not been proven that natural ventilation is always more energy efficient, and there is a risk of not sufficient ventilation in a sealed interior. The risk of failure is always apparent, as we have seen in the Netherlands. Therefore the logical order of solving things first in a passive manner and only then looking for active solutions, may not necessarily be the best approach when it comes to achieving sustainability targets. Careful design and development are needed.

However, things may change: intelligent management of installations will develop which will always offer more options for efficient energy use than natural systems.

Nevertheless, it is important to address this topic and to plan choices carefully. The main considerations in this area are the choice between a concept with or without cooling installations, and between natural or mechanical ventilation. ∎

- Lightweight envelopes and interior partitions are more likely to have noise problems due to airborne and structure-borne noise.
- Windbreaks outside (e.g., plants, trees) can cause security risks, providing hiding places for muggers.

Ventilation:
- An airtight envelope and inadequate ventilation control could cause poor indoor air quality. Poor ventilation is often the main reason for an unhealthy indoor climate.
- Opening windows for natural ventilation of houses could invite burglars.
- Air ducts and filters can become polluted with micro-organisms and create an unhealthy indoor climate.
- The electrical energy used by fans in mechanical ventilation systems can outweigh the benefit of good control. The noise they produce is often a reason why they are turned off.
- Low ventilation can cause too high radon concentrations. Radon emanates from the soil (depending on the site) and materials used, e.g., cement contributes greatly to radioactivity levels.
- Fire: insulation materials can be dangerous with fire.
- Balanced mechanical ventilation with heat recovery is potentially highly energy-saving. By opening windows, however, this effect is reversed.
- Because there can be problems with balanced mechanical ventilation, a well-controlled natural or hybrid (exhaust only) ventilation system is often preferred.

But if both a cooling system and a heating system are needed, a Heating Ventilation and Air Conditioning system is the obvious choice. However, the size of the system and its components means that computer simulation tools should be used. The installation also requires a high level of skill.

LINKS with other topics

The comfort levels selected, of course, greatly influence the energy-demand. In recent decades increasing comfort levels in the Netherlands have led to more energy demand, which has been offset by more efficient conversion tecnologies and new types of installation compnents. The overall energy demand for new-built housing has been lowered, despite this comfort growth.

Here too, avoiding problems and avoiding energy/materials input is a potential strategy, requiring better design skills by architects, supported by technological developments and a well-designed installation concept. This has been achieved through continuous knowledge transfer to architects, the introduction of regulations and the switch to performance-based legislation to allow for flexibility in the design and installation choices made (see also the chapter on legislation and energy).

The comfort concepts and supporting installation measures have increased materials use: larger radiators, double and triple glazing, sometimes heavier constructions. The switch to double and triple glazing has, however, helped to support outside noise level reduction requirements and to increase thermal comfortby the higher glazing surface temperature. ■

Acoustics and noise nuisance
Some history

The demand for airborne and impact sound insulation dates from the 1950s. Densely-populated urban areas, combined with a desire for privacy required standards for sound insulation. The oldest Dutch standard, NEN 1070, Noise Control in Dwellings, setting out these requirements, dates from 1962. Requirements were formulated for four octave bands only: 250, 500, 1000 and 2000 Hz centre frequencies. It contained two quality classes, with a difference of 3 dB in the requirements for airborne and impact sound insulation.

This standard was revised in 1976. Apart from the introduction of different units in which the airborne and impact sound insulation were expressed and a new reference curve for impact sound insulation, some new requirements were added:
- Maximum sound levels in dB(A) for building services;
- A minimum level of sound absorption in common areas like staircases, halls, and corridors, etc;
- Airborne and impact sound insulation between rooms inside dwellings;
- All requirements were formulated for five octave bands, with the addition of the 125 Hz octave band.

Nieuwland noise bund made from recycled construction materials
Source: Ronald Rovers

These new requirements were later added to the Building Decree (Bouwbesluit). By 1979 noise nuisance was seen as a serious problem in the Netherlands, noise , with a rapidly growing economy causing more traffic (and traffic noise) and, since it is a small country, new housing and other developments were increasingly close to connecting roads. This called for careful spatial planning and a revision of the acoustic and noise regulations. Therefore, the first Noise Abatement Act was passed in 1979. As a consequence of this, standards for the sound insulation of façades were introduced in building regulations, like the Building Decree. In this decree the noise levels from roads, railways, aeroplanes and industry is determined by means of standard calculation methods. Today every dwelling must meet the requirements laid down in the Building Decree. This is a minimum acoustical quality standard. By 1999 the third version of NEN 1070 was published. It includes the requirements for:
1. Airborne sound insulation between and inside dwellings;

2. Impact sound insulation between and inside dwellings;

3. Sound insulation of façades (against outdoor noise);

4. Noise from building services;

5. Reverberation in common spaces in multi-family dwellings.

Five quality classes of acoustical comfort were also introduced in these five areas. The middle class represents the same quality as in the Building Decree. The difference between the classes is 5 dB in sound insulation and noise from building services. These quality classes have not been included in the building regulations, so only the minimum quality laid down in the Building Decree is mandatory. A few years ago, the requirements for impact sound insulation were by 5 dB to achieve a better balance in quality between airborne and impact sound insulation.

Sound Regulations

At the moment of writing, Dutch legislation sets the following standards that design and construction must meet, expressed in international units. These standards provide the parameters for the conceptual design.

...

2.1 Airborne sound insulation

2.1.1 Between dwellings

R$_A$ >52 dB; sound reduction index weighted to the pink noise spectrum.

2.1.2 Between rooms inside dwellings

R$_A$ > 32 dB; sound reduction index weighted to the pink noise spectrum.

2.2 Impact sound insulation

2.2.1 Between dwellings

L$_{nTA}$ < 54 dB; the spectrum of the tapping machine is weighted to a reference spectrum which is −15 dB in all octave bands.

2.2.2 Between rooms inside dwellings

L$_{nTA}$ < 74 dB; the spectrum of the tapping machine is weighted

to a reference spectrum which is −15 dB in all octave bands.

2.3 Sound insulation of facades

The background to this requirement is that noise levels inside dwellings caused by outdoor noise should not exceed 35 dB(A). Until now the unit used is (translated):

R$_A$ > the level of incident noise − 35 dB(A)

The level of incident noise on the façade is determined according to the prescribed calculation method laid down in the Noise Abatement Act.

2.4 Noise from building services

The A-weighted level of building services should not exceed 30 dB(A). This applies to toilets, water taps, elevators, boilers, and ventilation.

2.5 Reverberation in common spaces

Reverberation is controlled by installing a minimum amount of absorption in these areas.

The total sound absorption A in m2 should be equal to or greater than 1/8th of the volume of the room. This results in a reverberation of about 1.3 seconds according to Sabine's law.

LINKS with other topics

Dutch lessons in preparation of a new project
Some of the consequences of this legislation on acoustic comfort levels are:
• we now see in the Netherlands noise bunds erected between roads and built- up areas;
• provisions in windows (suskasten: windows

with sound-insulating ventilation openings);
• planning difficulties when looking for new sites to build on;
• consequences for timber frame builing. ■

1073741824

Light

Daylight is the basic source of light in dwellings and a design which gives optimum daylight saves energy. Windows also provide a view of the outside world. People are aware of the weather and feel less shut in. In order to experience the outside world there must be enough characteristics of the outside, e.g. the luminance must be sufficiently high and the sky must not be obstructed by surrounding buildings. Having a view of sunny surroundings is highly appreciated.

Short history

The dwellings built in the Netherlands in the 1950s and '60s had often living rooms with large windows at the two opposite ends. In this way sunlight was guaranteed irrespective of the orientation of the house. The building regulations at that time also had corrections for other buildings obstructing the access of daylight. The required daylight access was dependent on the use of the room (living room, bedroom, and kitchen). The results of the Bitter study were used in the old housing value rating system of 1962:
- 'Acceptable': at least 2 hours of sunshine between 19 February -- 21 October;
- 'Good': at least 3 hours of sunshine between 21 January -- 22 November.

The present

The building regulations now require a minimum daylight opening calculated using a prescribed calculation method. In this method corrections are made for obstructions from the building itself. The obstruction caused by neighbouring buildings, however, is neglected. One exception is the city of The Hague where sunshine is a topic in urban planning: sunshine in dwellings, critical urban areas as semi-public spaces for recreation. Other municipalities sometimes ask for a solar study especially when high-rise buildings are planned. This is increasingly happening. The tools for evaluation are available, but the criteria are not clear or uniform. Extending the regulation to cover solar radiation in urban planning could solve this problem.

Effects of sunlight

A Dutch survey (Bitter, 1961) among the residents of a dwelling showed that two hours of direct sunshine between 0800 hours and 1600 hours on the 19th February was classified as 'moderate' and at least three hours sunshine between 0900 hours and 1500 hours on the 20th January as 'good'. In the classes moderate and good there are few complaints. Seventy percent of the respondents preferred a bad but sunny view, to a nice view in the shade. The results are confirmed by studies abroad and can be regarded as valid for the temperate climate zones. In a German study the majority were only positive about the sunshine duration if it was longer than 5 hours in March. Briefly, the positive effects of sunshine reported in the literature are:
• Biological and therapeutic effects: this should be related to UV radiation, but as this is blocked by glazing it is not very clear;
• Heat gain (passive solar): the radiant heat gain is very much appreciated in the cold season (see section on energy);
• Visual effect: as lighting levels increase, the correct use of sunlight will decrease energy consumption for lighting. However direct sunlight will often be blocked to avoid glare. Positive effect is the contrast of light and shadow in rooms with direct sunlight.
• Psychological experience: this can be considered as the most important factor. This is also true for the areas adjacent to the building: terraces with sun in the intermediate seasons, dwellings with south-facing balconies and gardens sell the best. ■

Artificial light

Artificial light is becoming more and more efficient. People are also increasingly using artificial light to create a particular environment. The technical development of lighting systems and their control is a major topic for the future. Anticipation of this will have little impact on the building design but it will affect the energy consumption.

> Outdoor comfort
Urban comfort

In the Netherlands we see a growing trend towards outdoor recreation over a longer period of the year, while the climate in our country only allows for limited periods in which outdoor activities can take place in comfort. In some cases this places a greater burden on our resources, e.g. gas heated outdoor terraces. Nevertheless, there is a direct relationship between comfort and how the urban structure is developed which can improve the situation without directly influencing environmental performance. Other aspects of growing importance are safety and pollution which require a sound approach to the outdoor environment to avoid problems. Comfort and health depend on the properties of the outdoor environment. These properties are changed by a building, the geometry of outdoor spaces and the structure of the town as a whole. Some of the properties that change are: the spread of air pollution, heat radiation, shadow, wind, daylight, temperature (heat islands), humidity (town), precipitation (town), and noise. Sustainable design also means designing an outdoor environment which is comfortable and healthy.

Urban comfort: even when we are outdoors we like to improve our comfort nowadays
Source: Ronald Rovers

Wind

In the cold season wind will cause discomfort. At the corners of high-rise buildings it can even be dangerous. In the warm season wind may have a positive effect on comfort but even then, the negative aspects of wind are considered more important. In the Netherlands a variety of criteria for the evaluation of wind comfort has been in use for several decades. A wind comfort criterion defines the wind conditions in urban spaces where people will experience comfort or discomfort because of the wind. People in urban spaces include the general public as well as specific groups like the elderly and children. Urban spaces vary from shopping centres to parks, car parks and paving.

Recently a committee agreed on criteria to be used in future. Three classes are accepted for separate assessment: business walking in traversing areas, pedestrian walking in launching areas and sitting/standing. For all these classes the same threshold wind speed applies: 5m/s. The permitted probability of exceeding this value depends on the activity class and the quality class chosen i.e. good, moderate or poor. For danger, a threshold of 15m/s applies with 4 quality classes for the probability of exceeding (no danger, 0%; acceptable, tolerable and dangerous, 0.5%). In the planning phase of a project, the wind comfort has to be evaluated, using a wind tunnel. No expert is necessary if the following statements are true:
1. The building is less than 15m high and has no open passage under it.
2. The building is less than 10m high or is less than 50% higher than the surrounding buildings.
3. The building is not close to the coast.
4. The use of the outdoor space near the building is not sensitive to wind comfort.

Probability of exceedance as % of the total number of hours a year	Quality class	Activity		
		I Walking	II Strolling	III sitting
<2.5	A	good	good	good
2.5-5	B	good	good	acceptable
5-10	C	good	acceptable	bad
10-20	D	acceptable	bad	bad
>20	E	bad	bad	bad

Sunshine and shade

People use open places if they are sunny. Favourite outdoor spaces are on the south side of buildings. This has consequences for the planning of gardens and urban open places. The hours of sunshine can easily be predicted. However, it is difficult to evaluate the results because no generally accepted criteria for sunshine in urban spaces are available. The criteria will depend on the use of the space. For example, sunshine on a school playground is valuable, but only at the times it is being used. Some municipalities in the Netherlands now require a sunshine study for new urban plans and use the results, for example when solar collectors or photovoltaic cells are applied.

Air quality
Urgency
Air is life, and air quality has a direct impact on the quality of life in both the short and the long term. Not just people, but plants, animals, water, soil and buildings can also be damaged by poor air, and all organisms benefit from good air quality and natural smells. People with respiratory tract problems and cardiovascular disease in particular, are more sensitive to polluted air. –These health issues, ranging from slight discomfort to death, have a serious impact on both society and the Dutch economy. In the Netherlands more than 10% of the population suffers from respiratory disease and the medical costs involved are huge.

Estimated effect of anthropogenic PM2,5 on life expectation (months) in 2000, 2010 and 2020.

Poor air quality in the Netherlands currently causes loss of life up to three years per person which could be reduced by policy and technical measures in various sectors.
Source: IIASA

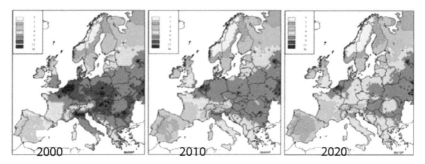

2000   2010   2020

Background
In 2000 McGranahan and Songsore presented a transition model in which they argue that every developing country or society will go through different stages of air pollution. All over the world many people are suffering from the effects of air pollution, but the sources and the risks are not the same everywhere. In underdeveloped countries, the main risks are caused by the use of wood or charcoal for heating and cooking ; women and children are especially vulnerable to this exposure.

When countries start to develop, all types of industry and traffic produce a lot of air pollution. In all societies, the rich are the first who are able to escape from unhealthy surroundings and to create acceptable microclimates in their homes, workplaces and cars. The poor suffer the most. Due to bad work conditions, they are subjected to air pollution from traffic and from manufacturing, and at home, they are subjected to the unhygienic conditions of poor housing. A modern developed society often manages to reduce air pollution from the combustion of fossil fuels in its own country (while at the same time increasing the damage in other

42

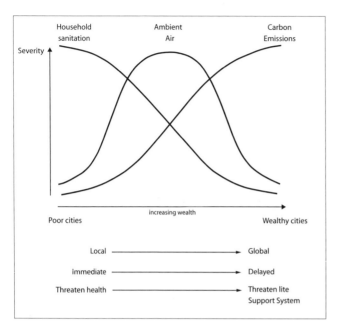

Severity

| Household sanitation | Ambient Air | Carbon Emissions |

Poor cities   increasing wealth   Wealthy cities

Local ———————————→ Global

Immediate ———————————→ Delayed

Threaten health ———————————→ Threaten lite Support System

Transition model
Source: McGranahan and Songsore

parts of the world), but new risks to air quality are introduced, like new chemical and biological substances.

The Netherlands has passed through all the stages in the transition model over the last 150 years. The so-called 'hygienists' in the latter half the 19th century, demanded that something be done about the poor living conditions of the lower classes. The Dutch Housing Act of 1901 is essentially based on public health, with many regulations to improve air quality, daylight and sewerage. It may be said that about hundred years of the Housing Act and the Building Decree have gradually managed to raise the general standards of the housing stock in the country to a very reasonable level of quality, including the climatic and air quality aspects. The Dutch building legislation provides regulations for minimum capacities of air supply and removal around different functions in the house. For many decades local government was responsible for inspecting these aspects in new and renovated housing, but this role decreased from 1990 onwards. Due to energy saving programmes, the natural and continuous infiltration of air diminished from 1980 up to the present period. Indoor air quality was largely neglected, with few regulations on this aspect. From 2000, various stakeholders, including the public health sector, urged that more attention be given to these issues. 2004 was declared the 'Healthy Indoor Environment' year. Although extra qualities are not the first concerns in mainstream contemporary house building, the topic 'air' has really become an item, with more and more professionals and consumers working towards construction and installation techniques that deliver better indoor air quality and improve other indoor environmental aspects.

Strategy

To promote clean air, efforts could best be targeted in three areas:
- Avoiding the emission of physical, chemical and biological emissions to the air;
- Cleaning or removing polluted and humid air;
- Keeping sensitive people away from places that could pose a threat to health.

Outdoor air quality

The first step in urban planning is to identify locations where the air is of sufficient hygienic quality, and where the air smells good. This means finding areas where emissions from industry, traffic and other activities are low or acceptable (in Europe NOx is used as an indicator, and the maximum year average is 40μg/m3), and preferably where there are open spaces with water and greenery. These sites are suitable for housing, schools, open air sports and other facilities where substantial groups of ordinary people, among them children, the elderly and pregnant women, will spend many hours a day. Finding acceptable surroundings for the average population is one thing, keeping them that way is another. There is a lot of evidence to show that it really makes sense to diminish emissions to the outdoor air as much as possible. Although the contribution made by each neighbourhood to the worldwide climate seems minor, to improve health quality on the spot it is worthwhile to reduce the combustion of fossil fuels, avoid open wood fires and control road traffic. This gives way to safe, quiet and clean microclimates, with energy systems like district heating or solar/wind techniques.

When housing has to be built in an area with air pollution, in theory it is possible to provide acceptable indoor air quality by using full air-conditioning, including air cleaning. These systems are expensive, need an appropriate design, and bring new risks and disadvantages. One of the risks is the growth of fungus and other micro-organisms in the humid filters, which then spread throughout the house. The disadvantages include the high energy consumption and the sound level of the systems in living rooms and bedrooms. And even if the indoor air is purified, residents will still be subjected to the polluted air outside the house when they spend time outside gardening, jogging, playing or doing other activities.

Multifunctional use of space in a densely-populated country like the Netherlands creates conflicts between indoor and outdoor conditions.
Source: Frans de Haas

Recommendations - summary of indoor/outdoor comfort following DCBA method

NB: measures at a higher level include or replace the measures at lower levels

Item	D	C	B	A
Clean site planning	On the brink of national and international legislation and regulation	New housing areas some distance away from high-risk activities (traffic, industry, waste dump, etc.)	• All housing only in spots > 200m from motorways • Avoiding areas with much pollen	• Maximum separation of clean and polluting activities in regional and urban planning • Transition of road networks to spare residential districts from air pollution • Protection of areas with fresh air and good smells
Outdoor pollution (neighbour-hood)	Contemporary use of space, cars, fires, etc.	• Centralised car parking • Individual high performance heating installations • No open fires outside or inside • Playgrounds and sports facilities in cleanest parts of the district • Regular waste collection	• Priority to slow traffic • Collective high performance heating installations • Low-allergen greenery • Practical and clean provisions for collective waste collection	• No cars in the neighbourhood • Free and safe bike parking sites • No combustion of fossil fuels (heatnets, solar energy, full electric) • Nice smelling gardens
Indoor pollution	• Contemporary use of equipment, carpets and furnishings, toys, glues, etc. • Water-soluble paints • Masking of smells and odours • National regulations for product quality and safety	• Individual high perform-ance installations and equipment • High quality carpeting, furnishings and interior elements • No masking of smells	• Collective high per-formance installations • Less domestic equip-ment • Breakdown of smells	• No combustion of fossil fuels (heatnets, solar energy, small scale wind energy, full electric apparatus) • Natural and fully non-suspect interior furnishing materials • No burning of candles, incense, etc.
Moisture	Watertight construction according to building regulations	• Extra insulation of ground floor against moisture and cold • Water-saving shower No humidifier	• Compartmentalised and closed arrangement of bathroom and kitchen • Warm ground floor and heating preferably by low-temperature/radiation • No overcrowding of rooms (e.g. bedrooms) • No aquarium, other water surfaces and water activities indoors	• Compartmentalised and closed arrangement of bathroom and kitchen • Full low-temperature heating systems in flooring and/or walls • Water-saving technology • Hygroscopic building materials (as regulators) • Everyone has their own bedroom
Ventilation	• Building Decree • Normal techniques • Extras only added due to energy-regula-tions, but as little as necessary	• Simple version of high performance ventilation with heat recovery or 'intelligent' natural systems • Extra attention to adjust-ment and maintenance	• High quality and full adaptations of high performance ventilation with heat recovery or intel-ligent natural/ mechanical system • Certified installation work	• Maximum built-in provisions • Hybrid systems with full range of options • Certified installation work and maintenance
Conditions for hygienic behaviour	Hardly any	Good detailing: no acute angles and ledges, closed wardrobes, etc.	• Built-in vacuum cleaning system • Tidy hand-over of house • Practical provisions for waste collection (indoors)	• Built-in vacuum cleaning sys-tem with full set of accessories • Smooth finishing of walls • Collective/underground sewerage or waste

Indoor air quality

Indoor air is continually polluted by many physical, chemical and biological sources:
• Incoming chemicals, dust, moisture, odours, insects, pollen and other things from outside, including from the soil;
• Moisture and smells from cooking, bathing, breathing, plants and other things;
• Emissions and odours from building materials, carpets and soft furnishings, electrical household equipment and interior elements;
• Emissions due to human behaviour, such as tobacco, cosmetics, cleaning fluids, hair and skin particles, plants and pets, glue and paints, etc.

More than pollution in the urban space, poor indoor air quality causes many physical complaints, especially in sensitive people. Scientific research has shown that it can be a causal factor in asthma in children. A modern concern is the health threat caused by chemical emissions from materials like vinyl and fibreboard.

The level of emissions should be reduced as much as possible. During the development of housing, designers can contribute to this by choosing non-suspect materials and by creating the conditions for healthy behaviour, for example, by providing built-in vacuum cleaning systems.

Ventilation systems

A house always needs ventilation to remove moisture, toxins and pollution, and to let in fresh air. A good ventilation system provides a continuous exchange of air between the inside and the outside at a quite basic level, combined with extra capacity to remove very moist or polluted air in a short time: e.g., after showering, while cooking, to refresh bedrooms, or after parties. In a well-insulated house appropriate ventilation is not always a matter of course. It should be purposely designed, not just from a theoretical or technical point of view, but also in a way which is understood and correctly used by the residents. Three types of ventilation systems have been applied in the Netherlands over the last twenty or thirty years.
1. Natural input and natural output. This principle is based on straight air flows through all rooms and the house as a whole. Very few contemporary houses in the Netherlands are designed with a fully natural ventilation system.
2. Natural input in every room with mechanical output, usually centralised. This is the system most often used, with many high and low tech versions. Good technologies are available, but the usual system is often inadequate.
3. Mechanical input and mechanical output combined with heat recovery. The market share of these systems is on the increase, but technical developments are still needed. Full air-conditioning is the final step in this process.

Lately a new principle has been introduced: the hybrid ventilation system. The slogan for this principle is: "natural when possible, mechanical when necessary". This more complex system combines all the advantages of natural and mechanical systems, and tries to deal with the disadvantages. For the resident it provides a healthy indoor environment with good air quality, pleasant thermal comfort, clear and manageable settings and low energy costs.

Reshyvent system. The Reshyvent system is produced by a Dutch consortium that took part in a European research project on hybrid ventilation systems.
Source: Alusta

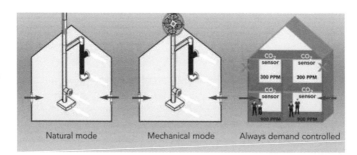

CASE STUDY

In Barendrecht/Rotterdam 40 low-allergen houses were built by Com. Wonen housing asociation. The trees and other greenery in the neighbourhood produce little pollen.
Source: Ger de Vries

Low-allergen housing
As a result of an initiative by the Rotterdam Municipal Health Service and VL Wonen housing association, 40 low-allergen houses were built in Barendrecht, near Rotterdam, in 2003. The compilation of the technical programme was supported by many specialists. The Health Service selected families with children suffering severe asthma and guided them through the processes of building completion, decoration and maintenance. Among other things, the indoor air quality has been monitored with research and the results are better than expected. Based on all the results, a checklist has been drawn up to help other projects. The measures are targeted towards a dry climate, dry construction and easy-to-clean surfaces and details. Examples from the checklist include:

• Good thermal insulation;
• A separate kitchen, with a direct outdoor connection;
• Floor-heating system on low temperature;
• High capacity ventilation system, with practical and comfortable operating facilities;
• A built-in vacuum cleaning system.

The houses were built for the public housing (rental) sector. The extra costs of about EUR 7000 per house, have been paid by the municipalities of Rotterdam and Barendrecht. National funding could not be obtained because of the special nature of both the building and the health aspects. The fact that 2004 was dedicated to indoor environment quality may in due course provide a solution to this financial problem. ∎

3 Resources

Water

Introduction

For centuries the Dutch have battled the water and tried to control it. Most of the old windmills for which the country is famous were built to pump water out of the built environment. Several circumstances have contributed to a change in this approach. First of all, it has been accepted that living with water is better than fighting it. Several river floods over the last decade have influenced this line of thinking. Second, climate change is causing sea levels to rise – while much of the land is sinking due to oxidation of drained peaty soils - and controlling surface and groundwater at today's levels in the Netherlands (for a large part below sea level) would require huge investments. A third reason is that people are starting to appreciate water as part of their living environment.

Sustainable local water management

Traditionally, water was not a building issue. Surplus water (groundwater, rain water) is drained and transported out of the urban environment. Domestic water is supplied by a central grid system, used in the building, and collected for transport by sewerage systems to a distant wastewater treatment installation. The first attempts to integrate water into sustainable building projects were by reducing the volume used in the building or house. Further improvements were made by rainwater harvesting for domestic water use.

Currently, new insights and technologies are aimed at a local approach to the water cycle, including local storm water infiltration and decentralised wastewater treatment, as well as facilitating ground-water recharge and urban landscaping. In this way a local water concept is developed which is directly related to the urban and building design. Sustainable local water management follows good practice principles: keep water local, minimise water use, do not mix clean and polluted water flows and facilitate local reuse of water.

This is currently recognized and several new issues can now be explored to add to the conceptual development:

Windmills in the Dutch landscape. Water as a design/ social element becomes more important in Ducth housing.
Source: Ronald Rovers

48

Water in the urban
environment.
Source: Ronald Rovers

*Source:
Dura Vermeer Groep NV*

- Local storm water infiltration for groundwater recharge and city landscaping;
- Minimizing external water supply;
- Wastewater separation at source and local treatment and reuse of domestic wastewater.

Since water itself is a continuous resource (and therefore renewable) a closed cycle approach to water consists mainly of treating the polluting elements in the cycle at local level and for re-use as much as possible. Water can be seen as an in and outgoing stream in the neighbourhood, and in between it is used. The polluting elements added to the water should be removed before releasing it again to the mainstream. This way a continuous loop is possible.

Not only is water seen more and more as a local cycle, but it is also becoming increasingly important to people as a feature of an attractive neighbourhood. Planning water into the city through urban landscaping creates an attractive residential setting and enhances people's involvement and awareness with respect to water issues. Houses near water are sold for higher prices than those elsewhere. Over the past ten years, extensive experience has been gained integrating water into the built environment in the Netherlands, resulting in a large number of innovative building projects.

Theme 1: Local rainwater
Storm water or rainwater provides an important water resource for cities. It is fit for groundwater recharge, city landscaping, industrial and household use. However, in many cities around the world, rainwater is directly transported out of the city area by sewerage or drainage systems and is discharged in downstream surface waters. This means that it is no longer available to the city. It is increasingly recognized that this is not a desirable approach, since city groundwater levels are often declining. Moreover, city sewer systems regularly have insufficient capacity to deal with the high volumes of extra water that are conveyed through the system – especially during heavy rain – often resulting in uncontrolled discharge of sewage through storm water overflows.

Local rainwater management requires a well-balanced design of the neighbourhood. During storm water events the water intensity can be high. Therefore measures need to be taken to optimise the local water holding and infiltration capacity. These measures are partially dependent on the geo-hydrological situation of the building area (soil type, groundwater level). Examples are water-slowing measures on roofs and special infiltration trenches. There should be sufficient free surface available for infiltration.

Another important issue that has to be taken into account is the quality of the storm water. Storm water is generally very clean, though rainwater flowing off intensively used roads might result in pollution. The storm water from these roads

Rainwater-slowing
measures on roofs
Source: Ronald Rovers

Wadi
Source: Ronald Rovers

can be cleaned (e.g., by reed bed filters) before being discharged into local surface water or in the soil.

In the Netherlands there is an increasing focus on local rainwater management. The aim for new building areas is that at least 60% of rainwater be 'uncoupled' from the sewer system, and preferably more. A great deal of experience, examples and creative solutions are available in a growing number of new and existing settlements.

Theme 2: Minimizing external water supply

Minimizing household water use

The initial attempts to improve the urban water system were by reducing the volumes of water used in the household, both by creating awareness and by installing water-saving equipment. Some examples of water-saving equipment are:
- Water-saving toilets (6 l / 3 l per flush);
- Water-saving washing machines and dishwashers;
- Showers instead of baths;
- Water-saving showers;
- Low-flush vacuum toilet systems (1-2 l per flush).

Rainwater harvesting for use in households

Rainwater harvesting for use in households can be achieved by collecting rainwater from roofs and piping it to storage tanks or to local water basins. Rainwater harvesting is relatively low cost, requires simple constructions and easily-obtainable construction materials. Rainwater is generally accepted as a good source of water for toilet flushing, washing machines and gardening. There are numerous examples where this application has been used.

Depending on the rainwater storage capacity installed, rainwater could replace 25-50% of the total water consumption in households.

Theme 3: Local treatment and reuse of domestic water

Domestic wastewater is an important local source of water that can be used for groundwater recharge, landscaping and various other purposes (e.g., washing cars). More than 130 m3 of wastewater is released per household per year.

The general strategy in closing the water cycle is the same as for materials and energy (i.e. based on the *Trias Ecologica* principle): reduce the need, use renewables, and meet the remaining need as efficiently as possible. The first two have limited effect. Although significant water savings can be achieved, water will be always needed. The only renewable local natural resource is rainwater, but its use for household purposes is limited to toilet flushing and washing machines. The main contribution comes from the third part: efficient treatment. And this requires local measures: separation of different water qualities at source, local treatment to avoid

Reed fields, Rosmalen
Source: Roos Berendsen

DCBAs for the three themes

NB: measures at a higher level include or replace the measures at lower levels

	D	C	B	A
All themes	External water supply (piping system) and direct discharge of rainwater and wastewater through sewer system	• Minimization of water use • Local rain water use or infiltration	• Minimization of water use • Local rainwater infiltration or use • Grey water treatment and reuse	Complete local water cycle
Theme 1: Local rainwater infiltration and groundwater recharge	Normal (transport of rainwater out of urban environment by sewer systems)	40% of local rainwater infiltration	60% of local rainwater infiltration	100% local rainwater infiltration, including the water of intensively used roads
Theme 2: Minimizing external water supply	Normal (water use 125 - 250 l per capita per day)	Water saving (25-40% reduction)	Use of rainwater for flushing and cleaning (25-50% reduction)	Completely autonomous (no external water supply)
Theme 3: Local treatment and reuse of domestic wastewater	Normal (transport of domestic wastewater out of the city area with sewer systems)	Local treatment and reuse of grey water	Local treatment of black water	Complete local treatment of wastewater with the aim of reusing the water for landscaping, car washing, etc.

large transport distances (and pumping energy). Full closing of the cycle (level A) is still a target for the future, but many elements have already been developed and introduced in modern housing developments in the Netherlands.

The use of wastewater requires treatment which ensures public health and environmental safety. There are various options for treating water on a local scale. The most promising systems that can be applied are based on an 'Ecological Sanitation' approach, with separate collection of grey wastewater (from cleaning activities, bathing and showering) and black wastewater (toilet wastes).

Local treatment and reuse of grey water
The grey water of households (up to 75% of the total water use) is relatively clean and therefore easy to treat on a local scale. The treated effluent can be used for groundwater recharge or landscaping. There are various examples both in the Netherlands and in Europe where grey water is treated in reed bed systems. (In the Netherlands, such systems are used in Arnhem, Culemborg and Groningen). The treatment results of these systems are very good and can comply with strict European discharge standards. There are also successful examples of compact methods for grey water purification, such as bio-filters and membrane bio-filters.

The treated grey water from reed bed filters is often discharged into local water systems that have a function in urban design. Landscape architects who have been involved with grey water projects state that reed bed filters are considered as design elements in urban landscaping and that viewed in this way the extra cost of local grey water treatment is low.

Local treatment of black water
Toilet waste, known as 'black water', constitutes only 1-2 volume percent of the total wastewater stream, but contains more than 80% of the nutrients found in domestic wastewater and the vast majority of human pathogens, drug residuals and hormones. In black water collection, with or without a minimum quantity of flush water, the organic matter and nutrients that are present remain concentrated and can be used for energy recovery through anaerobic digestion and for reuse as agricultural fertilizer. Potential hazardous components such as pathogenic organisms and drug residuals can also be efficiently isolated and degraded.

LINKS with other topics

The theme 'water' has links with several other topics of importance in sustainable building. It relates to architecture and housing design, e.g. through the implementation of different plumbing and piping, the construction of rainwater storage tanks and the introduction of special roofs. It also relates to materials with particular reference to the materials used in roofing, plumbing and piping, e.g. the use of zinc, aluminium or copper should be avoided in order to prevent the pollution of rainwater with metal ions. Materials like PE are preferred. The theme of water has a special connection with urban planning. To integrate a local water cycle into an area, particular attention needs to be paid to the urban landscape design during the planning phase. For example, sufficient open space and special infiltration trenches are required for rainwater infiltration. The natural slopes occurring in the area should be identified and used in designing the rainwater system. When reed bed filters are used in urban design, green areas can be created which should be set aside in advance. ■

Local wastewater
treatment and reuse in
Flintenbreite: reed bed
filters for grey water
treatment, adjacent to
houses.
Source: Otterpohl

85

Examples of sustainable building projects with innovative urban water concepts

Ecological building project EVA Lanxmeer, Culemborg

The ecological building project EVA Lanxmeer, Culemborg, was completed in 2004. The area comprises 200 houses and a number of office buildings. The project is an example of integrated sustainable building and innovative urban landscape design features. The urban water system was given special attention, including 100% storm water infiltration, a complete local grey water treatment and reuse system, and integration of the water system in the urban landscape design. The area is located on top of a water extraction area, which required far-reaching measures in terms of protecting groundwater quality.

Urban design of the ecological building project EVA Lanxmeer, with a major focus on water.
Source: Stichting Eva, www.eva-lanxmeer.nl

Alterra office buildings, Wageningen

The Alterra office buildings at Wageningen University are an example of a project in which the water cycle played an important role, along with the desire to create an attractive working environment. Innovative measures were taken with respect to rainwater harvesting and 100% local storm water infiltration. The office building is characterised by its spatial design. The office garden forms the heart of the building and is irrigated with rainwater from storage basins that adjoin the buildings. Most work places have a panoramic view of the garden that is also used for meetings. Storm water from the surrounding roads is infiltrated through wadi systems.

Alterra office building with the interior garden that is irrigated with rainwater from storage basins adjoining the office.
Source: Wageningen University

Sewerless city settlement Flintenbreite

In the German city Lübeck on the Baltic Sea, a demonstration project with a 'sewerless settlement' was set up in 1997. This sustainable building project named Flintenbreite, comprises 117 houses. Innovative features in the urban water system include 100% local storm water infiltration and a complete local wastewater treatment system. In the houses grey and black wastewater are collected separately. Grey water is treated in local reed bed filters that are integrated in the urban design. Low-flush vacuum toilets (water use 0.7 litre per flush) are used to collect the black water. The use of vacuum toilets results in a water saving of 25% of the total household water use. The concentrated black water is transported through a vacuum sewer to an anaerobic digestion system that is situated in a central building. The biogas produced is mixed with methane gas which is then used in a CHP (combined heat and power) system for district heating and local electricity generation.

Materials

In medieval times, most houses in the Netherlands were constructed from 'natural materials', what we currently refer to as 'renewable materials': a fully wood house or a wood frame structure filled with willow branches and loam, wooden floors, and a

56

Traditional houses in The Netherlands constructed from 'natural materials'.
Source: Ronald Rovers

roof covered with reed. In agricultural areas these types of houses were still being used until about a century ago.

In cities, wooden houses posed too great a risk of fire, so they were banned. Façades has to be made of brick, roofs had to be covered with roof tiles or slates. The wealthy, who could afford it, started to build houses using fired products. At that time the bricks were laid in limestone mortar which was easy to remove when walls were dismantled, and the bricks could be reused. Later, limestone mortar was replaced by modern, strong cement. This prevents the re-use of bricks from demolition work. However strange it may seem, the Dutch method of house building today still has a lot in common with the way the Romans built 2000 years ago: fired bricks for walls, laid in cement mortar, wooden window frames and doors, a wooden structure for the roof, and clay-fired tiles to cover it. Traditionally, building materials were found in the vicinity of the building site. Bricks and roof tiles were made of clay from river beds, and wood was found in the local forests.

Today, the mineral materials still come from national raw materials, but most materials come from all over the world. Many prefabricated elements have been introduced:
- Floors made of concrete (partly due to noise reduction and fire prevention legislation);
- Aluminium and/or plastic window frames (for low maintenance);
- Façade-filling elements, including thermal insulation and window frames.

Building materials are usually selected on the basis of several criteria:
- For strength in construction;
- For colour and texture (to express the architect's vision);
- To keep rainwater out and heat in;
- To keep intruders out;
- To fulfil these functions over a long period without the need for maintenance.

Towards sustainability
Besides these criteria, the importance of the environmental impact of the use of building materials has increased in recent years and provided additional criteria for the selection of building materials:
- To prevent the depletion of raw materials;
- To prevent damage to the landscape because of the extraction of raw materials;
- Selecting materials with low emissions during the whole life cycle;

Tunnel oven
Source: HUWA baksteen

- Selecting materials with low energy consumption throughout the entire life cycle (from extraction to recycling);
- To prevent waste during extraction, production and in the demolition phase.

Initial attempts to implement these criteria in the building sector consisted of measures like:
- Avoiding the use of synthetic materials (emissions caused by burning in the waste phase);
- Avoiding the use of gravel (because of damage to landscape caused by digging gravel out of riverbanks);
- Avoiding the use of zinc for rainwater transport (because of emissions from zinc to the rainwater).

The present approach has evolved more in the direction of a conceptual approach, which integrates all the elements of a closed materials cycle: an approach which focuses on the entire lifecycle of a building and the materials used.
Maintenance and re-use of buildings are important aspects in reducing materials and energy consumption, as well as creating a complete recycling system at sector level to minimise the input of virgin resources. The use of alternative materials and improved manufacturing of products are two more elements. An example of improved manufacturing is the use of new types of ovens, tunnel ovens, to produce bricks. The efficiency of these ovens was improved between 1990 and 2000 such that 50% less energy is now required. By using natural gas, this results in fewer emissions and less air pollution. This sustainable innovation was supported by SenterNovem.

The policies pursued include:
- Stimulating the market to recycle:
    - By placing a ban on the dumping of construction and demolition waste which can be recycled or incinerated to produce energy (with associated measures, see box in the chapter on concepts);
    - By introducing environmental levies to increase the cost of dumping.
- Switching to agricultural-based products:
    - With policies to support more use of wood in construction and research on new agricultural-based products. Bamboo-based products are believed to have great potential for the future (www.agrodome.nl).

- Undertaking research to measure the precise environmental impact of using the different materials:
    - Not just the effects of the materials themselves, but also the amounts used in a building, to determine the effects on national and global scales.

In the Netherlands, about 150 million tonnes of building materials a year are used to build houses, offices and infrastructure, with only about 10 million tonnes being used for new housing. About 60,000 new houses (1% of stock) are built every year, with about 16,000 being demolished.

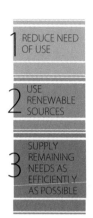

Strategy

To reduce the environmental impact of the use of building materials in *new* construction, the *Trias Ecologica* provides the main strategy (similar to the energy strategy):
1. Avoid the need for building materials;
2. Apply renewable sources;
3. Select materials with the lowest environmental impact.

To avoid the need

Avoiding the need for new raw materials for buildings can be done by:
• Prolonging the life of existing buildings and building products, e.g., through more flexibility in space and shape;
• Designing compact buildings, e.g., multi-level buildings or more houses in a row.

At stock level this means that when there is demand for housing, the following steps can be taken:
Step 1. Look for an existing building that can be used;
Step 2. Investigate whether an existing building can be transformed to fit the purpose;
Step 3. If steps 1 and 2 fail, a new building can be designed made from existing building products (reuse);
Step 4. If steps 1, 2 and 3 fail, a new building can be designed made from new building products, following the principles of the *Trias Ecologica*.

Renewable sources

There are two types of renewable building materials. Materials made out of agricultural products, i.e. 'natural materials', and products made out of recycled materials. By using agricultural products and products from recycled materials, a closed cycle of material use is created.

Natural materials

Timber is a renewable product. In the Netherlands it is used on a large scale. On a much smaller scale, cork and sheep's wool are also used, e.g. for thermal insulation. Coconut fibre is used for acoustic insulation and other organic fibre (flax) is

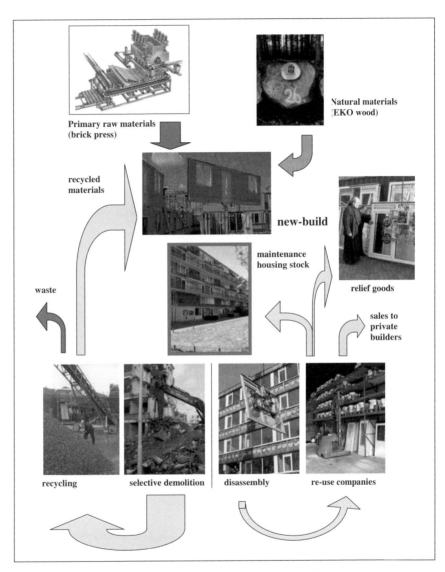

Primary raw materials
(brick press)

Natural materials
(EKO wood)

recycled
materials

new-build

maintenance
housing stock

relief goods

waste

sales to
private
builders

recycling   selective demolition   disassembly   re-use companies

Cycle of material use for
housing
Source: Frans de Haas

used in plate materials. Research is being carried out to develop new construction products of agricultural or organic origin.

Recycled materials
Up to 95% of mineral building and demolition waste is now re-used either as granulate for road foundations or to replace gravel in new concrete. Old PVC window frames and drain tubes are shredded and used as a secondary source for new PVC products.

The re-use of products (bricks, wooden beams, window frames) has just started to develop and further integration in the materials cycle has to be established over the coming years.

Lowest environmental impact

After applying the above approaches, there are still many different ways to use materials in built structures. There is always more than one solution available for built structures This provides an opportunity to select the solution which results in the least environmental impact.

A computer program has recently been developed in the Netherlands based on the *LCA (Life Cycle Assessment) method*. This software makes it possible to express the environmental performance of buildings as a figure or a set of figures. The program calculates the environmental impact throughout the entire life cycle of a building (from extraction of raw materials and construction, to exploitation and demolition). Environmental data on all the materials used in the building sector are held in a database. Data is collected about all the raw materials, about emissions, energy use and waste during the lifecycle of the products. The relevant data is then selected and the LCA calculations are carried out using an advanced computer program. The environmental impact of just one building material can be calculated or that of an entire building. The result of the calculation is a score for the main topics, and a total score. As early as the design phase, the program can reveal the performance of a building in terms of its sustainability.

LINKS with other topics

The relationship between materials and energy is obvious: energy improvements often require materials input, e.g. insulation materials are used for energy saving measures. Research has shown, however, that even when a very thick insulation package is used, the environmental benefit because of the saving of energy is much greater than the environmental impact of producing the insulation materials.

Health
There is a close relationship between materials and health. During the lifecycle of materials they give off emissions, some of which influence people's health. In the production phase, factory workers inhale the emissions. When houses are used, the inhabitants' health can be influenced by the emissions, and in the demolition phase, when part of the demolition waste is burned, people in the surroundings of the waste oven will also inhale the emissions.

Research has demonstrated which emissions are given off and their influence on health. Examples of known harmful emissions are:
• Formaldehyde (from chipboard, in the usage phase);
• Plasticizers (softener) in plastics;
• Dioxin (burning plastics in the demolition phase);
• Radon (from minerals).

Legal limits for emissions should therefore be set to provide a healthier indoor climate. Products need to be improved to guarantee healthier housing.

Design
There is, of course, also a close relationship between materials use and design. Many fragmented elements in a buildings design cause extensive materials use. More compact designs help to limit materials use.

Other design tools to reduce the material use include:
• The use of standard/prefab products (this also improves recycling opportunities after demolition);
• Designing for disassembly (this makes it easier to replace parts in the event of maintenance);
• Exploiting the special qualities of materials and avoiding over dimensioned structures;
• Using materials which do not need much maintenance during their lifecycle;
• Being aware of the environmental impact of materials before selecting materials for a building design. ∎

A practical approach

Besides a calculation system based on the LCA method, a more indicative method is used, the *DCBA method*, to guide new housing construction with the lowest possible impact. Using this classification system will enable different building concepts to be designed:

D: Normal selection of building materials based on construction quality, aesthetic quality and cost;.
C: Selection for sustainable building, avoiding the most serious environmental effects;
B: Minimising environmental effects;
A: 'Local' and organic building.

Building parts	Standard Concept D	C	B	A
Foundation	Concrete	Concrete with shredded stony demolition waste	Concrete with shredded stony demolition waste (granulates)	Concrete and sand-lime bricks
Ground floor	Combination of concrete beams, EPS insulation and concrete finishing	Prefab elements of concrete with shredded stony demolition waste	Prefab elements made of concrete with shredded stony demolition waste	Cellular concrete on sand underground
Store floor	Concrete	Hollow prefab elements of concrete with shredded stony demolition waste	Wooden platform frame construction	Prefab hollow concrete elements
Slanting roof	Wooden cassette	Wooden cassette with insulation of organic fibre	Wooden cassette with organic fibre insulation	Wooden cassette with organic fibre insulation
Roofing	Concrete roof tiles	Roof tiles made of concrete with shredded stony demolition waste	Roof tiles made of concrete with shredded stony demolition wast	EPDM with vegetation top
Façade	Outside: bricks Inside:prefab. concrete	Outside: bricks, Inside: sand-lime bricks	Outside: Wood Inside: Wooden platform frame construction	Outside: Concrete and bricks. Inside: Wooden platform frame construction
Window frames	Wood not from sustainable managed tropical forests	European wood from sustainably managed forests	European wood from sustainably managed forests	European wood from sustainably managed forests
Insulation	EPS or rock wool	Rock wool	Organic fibre and rock wool	Roof: organic fibre, Facade: sheep's wool
Construction walls	Concrete	Sand-lime bricks	Wooden platform frame construction	Sand-lime bricks
Internal walls	Gypsum blocks 70mm	Sand-lime bricks	Wooden platform frame construction	Loam stone (not headed) oven
Waterstops, tubes, etc.	Metals	Synthetic materials, PP, PP-R, EPDM	Synthetic materials, PP, PP-R, EPDM	Synthetic materials, PP, PP-R, EPDM
All wooden parts	Wood not from sustainably managed forests	European wood not from sustainably managed forests	European wood from sustainably managed forests	European wood from sustainably managed forests

62

Materials concepts for new Housing Based on the DCBA approaches

different building concepts can be developed.

Level D:
Normal selection of building materials based on construction quality, aesthetic quality and cost.

Why this concept?
• It has been the traditional way of build-ing over the last few decades;
• No special skills are needed;
• Meets the Dutch building legislation (no more, no less).

Level C:
Selection for sustainable building, avoiding the most serious environmental effects.

Why this concept?
• The aim is to reduce environmental impact only by choosing other materials;
• The materials are not very different from traditional materials but have a lower environmental impact;
• With a minimum of effort a more sustainable building is built.

What is needed?
• No special skills are needed, but the architect has to know what the environmental effects of the different materials are;

• Producers and dealers have to make an inventory of the environmental effects of their products during the lifecycle of the products and
provide that information to architects;
• Using materials sourced from demolition waste or made from natural materials improves the environmental quality of building products.

Level B:
Minimising environmental effects.

Why this concept?
• The wooden platform frame construction results in a lightweight building, built from materials sourced in the region;
• In the demolition phase the wood can be re-used as construction material or can be burned to produce heat for electricity;
• Less stony materials are used to create a healthier indoor climate;
• The wooden frames are prefab, so there is less waste in the production phase.

What is needed?
• Special attention needs to be devoted to noise reduction and fire prevention between houses;
• Special attention also needs to be given to the airtight connection between the different prefab elements;
• Parts of houses that could become

wet or moist have to be conserved against rotting.

Level A:
'Local' and organic building.

Why this concept?
• The wooden platform frame construction results in a lightweight building, built from materials sourced in the region;
• Loam stone and wood are materials that can be found in the region;
• In the demolition phase the wood can be re-used as a construction material or it can be burned to produce heat for electricity. Loam stone can be used for the production of new stone;
• Less stony materials are used to create a healthier indoor climate.

What is needed?
• An architect who can work with these types of materials;
• Special skills are required from the contractor. An ordinary contractor cannot handle loam stone and roofing with a vegetation top.
• Parts of houses that could become wet or moist have to be conserved against rotting.

CONCEPT D
onsite concrete construction Maasslu
Source: Frans de Haas

CONCEPT C
Steps of a multiple
story wood-frame
construction Aalsmeer,
Van der Breggen
Architects *Source:
www.centrumhout.
nl/hsb/webcam.html*

CONCEPT B
(right) Shredded stony
demolition waste.
Source for new concrete.
(left) Window frame
from a demolition
project. Reused in small-
scale renovation
project or PCV. Window
frame recycled for new
PVC and glass recycled
for new glass.
Sources: Frans de Haas

64

CONCEPT A

A-level office project: Headquarters for the regional waterways-authority (Terneuzen), among others based on timber frame and many recycled wooden products.
Source: Ronald Rovers

One of the few examples of A-level architecture by Renz Pijnenborgh
Source: Archi Service

Energy
Introduction
Until the 1960s, most Dutch houses were still heated by a central stove, using coal as fuel. There was one heated room in which everybody gathered on winter evenings. Since those days, change has been rapid. The growing demand for a healthier indoor climate, and the discovery of large amounts of natural gas in the Netherlands, created a massive demand for gas-fired central heating systems in Dutch houses. At first, the radiators in other rooms were shut off, and people still gathered in one heated room, but now that the whole house could be heated, the use of the house soon changed, with every room heated and used in winter (combined with more lights and, relative to income, cheaper electricity).

While this initially caused a huge increase in energy use, the energy demand for heating newly-built and existing houses has now been reduced from an average of 2500 m3 to 800 m3 natural gas per year, while preserving a good indoor climate and air quality as a combination of regulations and improved construction quality.

Electricity is the other main energy source for housing, and its use has been growing over the years: first because of the increased use of hot water and lighting, and later through the introduction of new appliances (e.g., dishwashers, washing machines); more recently, computers and additional hardware have made electricity consumption rise.

Strategy for energy-efficient housing
There are now many measures and techniques available to reduce energy consumption and CO_2 emissions in the built environment. Houses are designed to last a long period of time. Some lessons we have learned in this respect are:
- The most effective time to implement energy-reducing measures is when a new housing project is being constructed or a project is being renovated;
- Energy-efficiency is not just a technical issue, but an interaction between:
    - A smart energy concept;
    - The quality of house construction and installations (e.g., achieving the required air tightness as part of the energy concept);
    - The behaviour of the consumer. The attitude of the consumer determines whether an energy-efficient design really is energy efficient. (use of the ventilation system in the most energy-efficient way, and the number and the efficiency of appliances, such as refrigerators and computer hardware). This type of energy demand is growing and is not influenced by construction measures or legislation.

Anticipating for the future
The target in the Netherlands now is to construct zero-energy housing areas by the

year 2010. Experiments with zero-energy houses started in the 1990s. These are houses that can fully meet their energy needs from their own production. However, there is a shift in time: they produce more than needed in summer (via solar collectors and cells). The heat is stored in underground water aquifers for winter use and the electricity is passed back to the grid. In winter production is low, and the surplus is taken back from grid and storage. This principle can also be referred to as the zero-emissions concept, or CO_2 neutral concept, although there are some relatively minor differences between the two concepts. Over the years it has been seen that it is more effective, in terms of energy and cost, to implement these concepts at neighbourhood level rather than in a single building. Many devices to support these concepts are currently in development. Promising technological concepts include integrated wind turbines (on roofs) new, more efficient heat collectors and the integration of solar collectors in the asphalt roads of the neighbourhood.

It is not feasible for this concept to be applied in all new-built houses in the near future. But by being aware of this concept, new construction can anticipate for this and make it possible for a future upgrade to this system to be added later. Therefore we think that it is important to have an idea of this future zero-emission energy concept and thus be ready to anticipate future developments and techniques. A truly sustainable house and neighbourhood has to be able to function for the next hundred years or so, especially the components with a long lifetime, such as the urban grid and the structure of the building. It is expected that in the next 20 years the cost of electricity generated by PV systems will become equal to the price of electricity taken from the grid. So people will want to install PV systems in the future. This is important in terms of the shape and orientation of the roofs we design today.

Another important decision for the future is the selection of the energy infrastructure. This discussion started only recently in the Netherlands. Over the next 50 years the Netherlands energy supply has to become CO_2 neutral, especially in residential areas. When choosing an energy infrastructure today we have to consider the possibility of shifting from natural gas to a CO_2-neutral energy supply (e.g. hydrogen or biogas).

Energy efficiency and sustainable energy measures

The energy efficiency of housing is expressed in national legislation as the EPC (Energy Performance Coefficient) of a building. In new housing projects, the local authorities are important players. They are jointly responsible for the implementation of the Dutch Kyoto agreements. At the start of a new building development the local authority negotiates with the project developers and housing associations on how to realize these climate targets. During this process several possible energy concepts are proposed and calculated in terms of energy efficiency and cost. But, as explained elsewhere in this book, efficiency and cost are not the decisive factors. Energy and sustainability measures also have synergy with other requirements, e.g. the level of comfort, architectural design and organisational aspects.

Supply chain .
Source: Ecofys

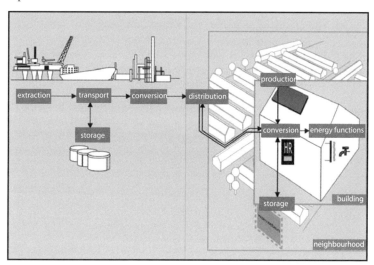

Trias Ecologica

In the next section we will present some integrated energy concepts based on the principles of the *Trias Ecologica* strategy:

Step 1: Reduce the (energy) demand. Energy that is not needed does not have to be generated. Points of interest in this first step are lowering thermal losses by insulating the building, reducing ventilation losses by means of heat recovery, and including sun shading to avoid overheating in summer.

Step 2: Use sustainable (energy) resources. Only sustainable energy should preferably be used to meet the remaining energy demand. For example, solar energy from thermal collectors or PV (Photovoltaic), or energy from ground sources and wind energy;

Step 3: Use fossil-fuel (energy) resources in the most efficient way.
Sustainable energy is not always available. Most of the renewable sources are dependent on: the time of the day (solar energy), the weather (wind), or the time of the year (solar energy). Energy from sustainable sources is also generally more expensive. So we still need energy from fossil sources, such as natural gas. This has to be used in the most efficient way, by high performance boilers or in heat pumps.

As explained in the chapter on building regulations, energy efficiency legislation in the Netherlands evolved from strict minimum measures to an integrated energy performance calculation method (EPC). This conceptual structure gives project developers and architects more flexibility in the design of a specific location and to meet the needs of the target group. Here we will introduce the state-of-art measures and techniques in the Netherlands: the ingredients that make up the concepts (menus).

Urban fabric level

Sustainability of energy concepts has to be taken into account in the urban planning phase of a project:
- *Passive solar energy:* large windows in the south façade and atria give natural sustainable heating of the dwelling, but the glass surfaces can cause overheating in summer. So both situations have to be considered. Overhangs or blinds are suitable sustainable measures to prevent overheating.
- *Active solar energy:* solar thermal collectors and PV generate hot water for heating and electricity. They give the best performance when located on the south side at an angle of 20-35 degrees. Roofs of houses are the perfect location for these systems. With the right roof shape, the best performance and the best architectural quality will be achieved.
- Apart from solar energy measures in individual houses, the urban structure also provides opportunities for the use of PV and wind systems, as the figures show.

Individual housing level
Building Level

Step 1: Lowering energy demand
- *Design measures:* position of windows, shape of the roof, overhangs, the floor plan (cold/ warm zone). For most of these measures the architect is dependent of the work of the urban planner;
- *Building mass:* the construction material (concrete or wood), i.e. the thermal mass of a building, determines the reaction to differences in the outdoor climate during the day and at night. There is a close relationship between thermal mass and the

LINKS with other topics

Energy is consumed to create a comfortable indoor climate. In the remainder of this chapter we will introduce a strategy and measures to reduce this energy demand. The subject energy is related to many other chapters throughout this book.

Indoor climate. The initial energy reduction campaigns started in the 1970s due to boycotts and rising oil prices, led to the introduction of insulation, double glazing and better air-tightness to reduce ventilation losses. At first this also created problems due to too little ventilation resulting in humidity problems. So there is a close relationship between energy-efficiency measures and the indoor climate, as explained in the chapter on comfort.

Architectural design. The architect and the urban planner make the first decisions that influence energy demand. For example, the use of passive solar energy in the wintertime, or the design of shading devices to keep the sun out in the summertime.

Building materials. Energy is also incorporated in building and installation products as well. Clearly to achieve better insulation or have more installations, more energy and more raw materials are needed to produce these components. An LCA (Life Cycle Assessment) gives an overview of the energy demand of a house during its lifetime, including the production and demolition phases.

In the Netherlands around 80% of the total energy demand is consumed during the occupation of the house and 20% in the construction and demolition. ∎

installation concept.

- *Insulation:* façade, glazing, roof, floor. These measures have a major impact, little
  maintenance cost and a long lifetime. In the Netherlands 120 mm mineral wool
  is standard (K=0.3), but in northern European countries twice as much is normal.
  Glass surfaces give the highest thermal losses. In the last 10 years, double-glazing
  improved with special coatings have improved K-values of up to 1.1. Even triple
  blade glazing is now available, but still very expensive.
- *Heat recovery:* besides thermal losses, the heat losses caused by the ventilating the
  dwelling can be reduced. A good ventilation system is needed to ensure a healthy
  indoor climate. Ventilating systems with heat recovery extract up to 95% of the
  energy in exhausted air and warm up the incoming fresh air. A fairly new
  technique is a heat recovery unit in the shower, a simple device that reduces 30%
  of the heating of warm water.
- Not included in the building regulations, but also very important is the energy
  consumption of electrical appliances. While the heating demand in dwellings
  is decreasing, the electricity demand is increasing. Energy labelling encourages
  consumers to buy the most efficient (A-label) appliances.

Step 2: Renewable energy

As already mentioned, a house is a perfect location for an active solar system, i.e.
close to the actual consumption, with little losses. The next sustainable source used

Measures at urban fabric
level: PV-lamp posts and
an urban wind turbine.
*Source: Ecofys and Wonen
Breburg*

in the built environment is latent heat and cold from the ground, air, or water. Because they use these sustainable sources, heat pumps are very efficient appliances for heating as well as cooling. In The Netherlands whole new areas are being equipped with heat pumps. The houses share a ground source. Reservoirs some 50 - 200 metres below the ground (aquifers), are used to store heat in the summertime and use it in the wintertime.

Efficient energy supply

A major difference between the various energy-conversion techniques is the choice between individual heating (and cooling) systems or communal systems for a building block or even a district. Standard Dutch houses are equipped with a high efficiency gas-fired boiler (with almost 100% efficiency). In coming years, we expect individual electric heat pumps to take a larger share. The optional cooling function of the heat pump is an important advantage of this technique. For larger areas a district heating system with a biomass-fuelled combined heat and power plant (CHP) is an option for a fully sustainable energy supply. The criteria for selecting individual or communal systems are:

- *The density of the project.* Communal district heating systems are more efficient and cost effective in high-density areas or apartment blocks.
- *The surroundings of the project.* For instance: is there residual heat available from industry or a power plant that can be used in a district heating system?
- *Control is often a criterion, besides energy efficiency.* Individual homeowners want to have the energy system in their own house, while housing associations prefer communal systems, outside the houses.
- *Future improvements in sustainability.* It is much easier to change an energy system at block or district level or to change the fuel supply (e.g., from natural gas to hydrogen or biomass).

Shower heat recovery unit and individual heat pump with boiler.
Source: ITHO

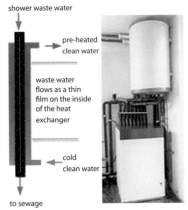

shower waste water

pre-heated clean water

waste water flows as a thin film on the inside of the heat exchanger

cold clean water

to sewage

Energy supply: Combined Heat and Power (CHP) district heating plant in Hannover, Germany.
Source: project brochure

Energy concepts
DCBA: 4 ambition levels

Examples of proven energy concepts, with four target levels, are presented in the following table. These four aspiration levels range from current building practice in the Netherlands to the zero-energy house. Some Dutch municipalities are aiming for zero-emission energy supply for housing areas by 2030-2050.

The graph to the right shows the four steps towards a zero-emission concept. The area in between the two lines (yellow & black) represents CO_2 emissions. The graph makes clear that in order to reach a zero emission situation, a growing amount of sustainable energy is needed:

- In the reference concept (D) the energy demand is fully supplied by conventional fossil fuel sources.
- At target level C, the energy demand is first reduced while sustainable energy is gradually increased, for example with a thermal collector.
- In the steps from C to B and from B to A it is implicit that the energy demand cannot be completely reduced to zero. Energy is still needed to operate the house and the appliances. More and more sustainable energy will be needed. This sustainable energy does not have to be generated right at the moment of consumption. Heat can be stored in boilers or even held in seasonal storage (aquifers), and the grid can be used as a storage system for electricity. The PV system on the roof of the house generates 80% of the annual production in summertime, while energy demand is low. In the wintertime we have the reverse situation. The concept is referred to as 'zero-emission' because the energy consumption is completely covered on an annual basis.

Energy concepts for DCBA targets

While PV is still expensive, the zero-emission status can be achieved by buying 'green' electricity generated by sustainable sources with greater cost-efficiency, such as wind turbines or hydro-power plants. The table on the next page presents some solutions for the four target levels. There are, of course, other options as well. One concept that is interesting is the low-tech passive house. In the progression from D to A the number of installations in the house grows. We need more and more installations for a very small energy demand. Installations are expensive, and have a shorter life span than building materials and need maintenance. The budget for installations could also be used to reduce the energy demand for heating almost to zero. Especially in areas with a lot of sunshine in the wintertime, passive solar energy provides enough heat to warm the house. This is called the passive house concept.

(left) Towards zero-emissions.
Source: Ecofys
(right) PV and solar thermal systems in Eva Lanxmeer
Source: Ronald Rovers

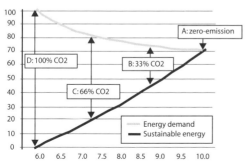

Eva Lanxmeer
Source: Ger de Vries

German example of a
passive house.
Source: Gussek Haus

	D	C	B	A
Urban and architectural design	Orientation: optional solar thermal and PV	Orientation: passive solar and solar thermal, option for PV	Orientation: passive solar, option for PV	Orientation: passive solar, option for PV
1: Energy demand reduction	Insulation K=0.3 (120 mm mineral wool)	Insulation K=0.3 (120 mm mineral wool)	Insulation K=0.25 (160 mm mineral wool)	Insulation K=0.2 (200 mm mineral wool)
	Double glazing	Double glazing	Double glazing	Double/ triple glazing
			Heat recovery	Heat recovery
2: Renewable energy		Solar thermal collector	Individual heat pump	Individual heat pump
		Passive Solar	Passive Solar	Passive Solar
			PV system (1 kWp)	PV system (4 kWp)
3: Efficient Energy supply	Condensing boiler	Condensing boiler	Individual heat pump	Individual heat pump
Energy performance	EPC 1.0	EPC 0.8	EPC 0.6	EPC 0.0
	1200 m3 gas	800 m3 gas eqv.	Wooden platform frame construction	Loam stone (not headed) oven
	3000 kWh	3000 kWh	5000 kWh (1000 kWh by PV)	4500 kWh (generated by PV)

Exampels of energy efficient projects.
Energiebalansstraat Leeuwarden (Zero-Emission street)
In 1996 the municipality of Leeuwarden started the development of two zero-energy or CO2 neutral projects. One of them is the 'Energiebalansstaat Pieter Christiaan Park'. The task was to develop a project that on a yearly basis covers the energy needed for heating and power, produced from sustainable sources.

Energy concept
The project demonstrates very clearly the principles of *Trias Ecologica* and the relationship between the design of the housing, the urban fabric and energy infrastructure. It is a project of 15 terraced houses of 150m2 on a piece of land stretching from North to the South next to the Van Harinxma Canal. The orientation of the location was not in ideal for using active and passive solar energy. The architect, Johannes Moehrlein, solved this by rotating the roof 90 degrees (like a saw).

The houses are very well insulated and equipped with a ventilation system with heat recovery. So the energy demand is very low (step 1). The energy supply is efficiently arranged with a communal gas-absorption heat pump system (step 3), which uses the energy from the canal nearby. The PV system and the canal provide the sustainable energy (step 2). The residents were also encouraged to make rational use of energy and consider buying efficient equipment (e.g. for kitchen, lighting). The project was closely monitored for a period of one year. In some houses the annual energy consumption was actually covered by the sustainable source. In other houses the electricity consumption appeared to be very high, far above the 2500 kWh/y that had been expected.

Energiebalansstraat project Leeuwarden, east façade and PV roof and solar thermal collectors.
Source: Ecofys

Zonnewoningen (Solar Houses)

In 1996 Ecofys, together with the World Wide Fund for Nature (WWF) initiated the Panda, or Solar Houses, project. Five of the largest Dutch project developers were approached with the request to develop houses that would need only half the amount of energy according to the national legislation. Secondly, the project should make use of solar energy and sustainable building materials, especially FSC (sustainably grown) wood. The project developers were allowed to use the WWF logo in their promotion. The project was a great success. The WWF label was effective in the marketing of the projects. It attracted clients, although the developments were more expensive. However, rising energy tariffs mean that a sustainable energy efficient house is a sound investment.

Energy concept

The project demonstrated that the requirements can be met with different architectural designs, from specifically solar architecture to traditional architecture, as the pictures show. The Solar Houses project meets target level C. From 2007 on this target level will become the standard in the Netherlands. The Solar Houses project proved that this target can be achieved on a large scale, in normal projects. In all the projects the principles of the *Trias Ecologica* were met. An energy concept with good insulation, ventilation heat recovery, a high-efficiency condensing boiler with a solar thermal collector was applied in most of the projects.

Solar Houses Eikenhage, Apeldoorn (left).
Source: Ecofys

Solar Houses, Wageningen (right).
Source: Katleen De Flander

4 Planning and Design

Urban Design

The UN Brundtland report "Our Common Future" was published in 1987, and between 1988 and 1995 several National Environmental Policy plans were drawn up. It became increasingly apparent that it was not just the building itself that was crucial, but that other areas across a wider scale influence the relationship between building and the environment. As a result, urban design started to change. Many sustainable options fall into categories like energy, water, materials, mobility and waste, across the whole spectrum of scales, from planology and urban design to architecture, building technology and installations to building details. Up until then we had seen attempts mainly to make improvements at building level, but not at neighbourhood or urban structure level.

In the daily practice of designing new housing projects, the most apparent modifications were seen in the area of traffic: after designing straight roads for several decades, neighbourhoods were designed to prevent non-local traffic taking short cuts, and to make the area more interesting by using curved roads. Over the last 15 years, this has changed as more aspects were taken into account in the urban design. Landscape and greenery became more important, as well as water. Initially, this was mainly for aesthetic and recreational reasons. Since the heavy rain in the winters of 1995 and 1996 with very high river levels and the danger of flooding, more attention has been devoted to water systems and how they are managed, including in urban areas.

The relationship between energy and urban design continues to be a difficult area. At the urban level, orientation towards the sun is important to enable architects to design houses and other buildings that can make use of passive and active solar energy. But most urban designers consider the solar orientation to be a severe limitation that they cannot handle.

For a long time ecological building and design has had an image of 'grass roofs, do-it-yourself building kits, and vegetable gardens.' Many 'modern' architects considered this to be the main obstacle when thinking about building and the environment. Fortunately, these two 'extremes' are evidently meeting halfway! Architecture offices such as OMA and Mecanoo have used vegetation roofs for a museum in Japan and the university library at the Delft University of Technology, respectively.

Urban Design issues
Water

Water is increasingly used as a structuring element in urban design in the Netherlands. For several reasons: firstly, because the Dutch love water and like to live close to it. Secondly, because local water is increasingly being used as part of the local water system, by decoupling it from the sewage grid and use local treatment. A third reason is that water management in the Netherlands as a whole is undergoing a major shift (partly due to climate change) and water buffering capacity is needed all over the country.

Energy

For energy the main consideration on the urban design scale is, as mentioned, solar orientation. Combining windmills for electricity production with housing areas is not yet very popular, despite the Dutch heritage of windmills. People like the low-tech historical mills but are afraid of noise and stroboscopic effects with the new high-tech windmills. The combined production of electricity and heat is increasingly used at neighbourhood level, along with aquifers 20 metres or more below ground to serve as storage and a source for heat pumps, which produce heat in winter and provide cooling in summer. The use of waste heat from industry and biogas from biological waste has just started. A tool, EPL (Energy Performance on Location), has been developed to calculate and compare the energy efficiency of neighbourhoods.

Materials

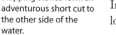

Stepping stones form an adventurous short cut to the other side of the water.
Source: Kees Duijvestein

In the area of materials there are not many links with urban design. It is rare for locally available materials to be used in the design. However, It is getting more common to integrate existing buildings and other structures into an urban plan to avoid demolition waste from the site and save virgin resources for new construction. In relation to water systems there is an ongoing discussion about the metals used in building, like lead, copper and zinc. The rain (acid rain in most cases) rinses off the metal surface and the metal particles are toxic to underwater life in water systems. Copper and lead are known problems, but there is a major debate between water experts and the building metal industry about zinc.

Landscape

Until 1980 it was common to take a blank sheet of paper to design urban areas

(tabula rasa). Particularly in low-lying wet areas, the tradition was to cover the existing landscape with a layer of sand (sometimes even three metres thick)! New ideas about the value of the existing landscape, structure and vegetation, as well as farms and other existing buildings has changed the approach to urban design. It is now normal to let the new plans fit into the existing landscape, to preserve cultural heritage as well as for ecological and recreational reasons.

Traffic

In more and more urban plans, routes for pedestrians and bicycles are being given priority. Between 1990 and 2000 it was thought that limiting the number of parking places would reduce car mobility. That did not work, because people wanted their cars (and their visitors' cars) close to their houses. Today the main approach is to provide parking garages to keep parked cars off the street.

A recent issue in Europe (April 2005) is the influence of motorised traffic on urban design. European rules about air quality prevent new housing and office areas from being built because they are planned too close to motorways, because of particulates and poor air quality. The Dutch National Institute for Public Health and the Environment (RIVM) has calculated that people living in areas close to motorways lose several years of their life. The debate on combining housing and working areas to prevent unnecessary mobility still has to be addressed.

Liveability and Safety

Liveability (quality of life) has been an issue for about ten years now; new political parties were even started on that theme in the mid-1990s. It began at local level and became national in 2000. Initially, liveability and sustainability seemed to be at odds with one another. It is now increasingly recognised that quality of life is an important aspect of sustainability. Safety is an important part of liveability. In

Tunnel for children in central park area and dragon as play element.
Source: Kees Duijvestein

some areas in Dutch cities, people do not feel safe. Safety has become a point of discussion particularly after the murders of two prominent individuals, a politician and a film maker, who had expressed strong opinions.

Affordability

In the Netherlands there has always been a good tradition of public housing for the more disadvantaged members of society, commonly referred to as 'social housing'. Often the more expensive properties have indirectly subsidised the construction of public housing. Since about 2000 this has occurred less, but even today, 20-30% of the newly-built housing is priced for this 'social' sector.

Good design: diversity and biodiversity

Dutch urban design has traditionally been calm and clear and well laid out. More recently, more spectacular designs have become popular, but considerable attention is still devoted to the quality of a design. Most municipalities have an Amenities Committee whose job it is to inspect the design quality of buildings (and sometimes the urban design too). Over the last ten years even developers have become much more interested in design quality.

Biodiversity: in an agricultural country with intensive bio-industry, the city may offer more room for nature. Diversity: over the last 50 years the planning tradition has been to keep housing, work and recreation separate from each other. This gives rise to more mobility (by car or by public transport), with the noise, pollution and accidents that this brings. Therefore the idea of combining functions at the urban level has become a new topic of discussion.

Wadi with bamboo
vegetation
Source: Kees Duijvestein

Health

Since 1976 there has been legislation on traffic noise nuisance which prevents building in areas where noise levels are too high. Until recently, other health aspects were not considered to be related to the urban design. But over the last few years health in relation to the built environment has received increased attention, including indoor climate, humidity, air quality, comfort and allergies since 1995, and since 2004, outdoor air quality (NOx, CO2, and particulates). In 2005, new European rules on levels of particulates in living areas made planners and politicians aware of the problem. In fact, several building projects in the Netherlands were postponed due to high levels of particulates.

The Urban design process
Interdisciplinary cooperation
Building teams generally consist of experts with various functions from various disciplines:e.g., municipal administrator, public official, developer, contractor, and external consultant. Possible disciplines may include civil engineering, town planning, architecture, landscape design, industrial organisation, and economics. Together they try to cover the whole building process. They have to decide on the conditions and concepts for the location regarding landscape, resources, comfort, health, traffic, and cross-border conflicts, etc.. Yet it often happens that certain subjects are inadequately dealt with because they do not come under any of the disciplines mentioned, or they are related to many disciplines and are only slightly covered per discipline. An interdisciplinary approach is needed to deal with this, supported with practical tools in the decision-making process.

The first step to such problems is to make the disciplines meet, often called 'multi-disciplinary' cooperation. The next step is interdisciplinary cooperation, in which participants venture across the safe borders of their own subject areas and occasionally try to think from the point of view of another subject area. This requires some insight into and appreciation of the other subject area. Interdisciplinary cooperation is very important in finding sustainable solutions.

Practical application:'Thinking in Systems, Designing in Variants'
Accomplishing an environmentally-sound design depends on all the partners involved in the design process. They will use their influence not merely on the basis of reason, but also and more especially, on the basis of the available finance and practical possibilities. To prevent the majority of environmental measures from failing during the building process, due to practical and financial objections, it is advisable to offer alternatives at an early stage in consultation with all the parties involved.

Tools and Methods
To bring all ideas and conditions to the table in a practical approach in order to define the concept is a highly complicated process, that requires a clear focus and broad mindset for integration in a clear set of guidelines for the design and a few underlying main drawings that mark the directions of development.

Over the years, a few tools have been developed that have proven to structure this process very well. The first (the DCBA approach) is to set targets and ambitions. The second (the site maximisation method) helps to create a preliminary outline for the construction site or urban development and to guide further, more detailed design. Both can be seen as part of the architect's "brief."

Theme	Sub Theme	D — The normal situation	C — Correction of normal usage	B — Minimise Damage	A — Autonomous
1. Energy	4000 natural gas equiv./househ./year	3000 natural gas equiv./household/year	2000 nat.gas equiv./household/year	only sustainable energy	
	1.1 generation	power station & gas-pipes	combined heat & electricity generation	sun and wind (heating and electricity)	seasonal storage
	1.2 building energy	10000 natural gas equiv.	7000 natural gas equiv.	4000 natural gas equivalents	local material
	1.3 usage	spreading of buildings	addition of sun lounge and storage	unbroken row of buildings in length, width and height	compact construction/ building
	heating	1300 natural gas equiv. (n.g.e.)	750 nat. gas equiv. (Overbos level)	450 nat.gas equiv., minimum energy concept	zero natural gas equivalents
	electricity	selec.pow.station;1000 n.g.e.=3000kWh	economical equipment, daylight 1500 kWh	no electric heating/cooking, 1000 kWh	limited usage; 500 kWh
2. Water	flush system			closed system	
	2.1 surface water	intake and distrib. to/from rivers	wetland treatment, storage and level fluctuations	seasonal storage, intake for extremes	no intake, complete purification
	banks	concrete wall, trop. hard wood timbering	shallow banks, timbering of natural materials	slope 1:8, 'timbering' reed/ vegetation	natural banks
	2.2 waste water	7 x per year flooding of sewer	separated sewer system	restrict need, vegetation roof/ rain barrels	disconnection of clean areas
	2.3 drinking water	supply according to demand (120L/p)	rain barrel in yards, water conservation (70 L/p)	use rain and surface water	supply from neighbourhood as well
3. Green	tabula rasa			building in existing landscape	
	3.1 land improvement	if need be, raise by fill overall	partial fill, save precious plants	fill under houses and streets only	no fill
	3.2 ecology/nature	small greenery; limited ecology	differentiated dynamic usage	make use of potential soil gradients	ecological infrastructure
	management	mow 8 times; spray insecticides	phased mowing, max. 2x year & removal	ecological management; sheep, cows, horses	natural balance
	3.3 recreational greenery	according to standards	greenery within walking or cycling distance	recreation within the neighbourhood	completely integrated
	3.4 food production	kitchen gardens as afterthought	educative value 20m2/housen. in neighbourhood	100m2/hh. crops and small livestock	>> 1000 m2 / household
4. Living/Work environm.	work opportunity	residential housing v. office parks	several dwellings with office space	clean industry and offices within the neighbourhood	teleworking local centre
	4.2 services	concentrated at neighbourhood level	services within walking or cycling distance	several small scale services within the neighbourhood	small scale services
	4.3 occupant behaviour	slow changes in behaviour	changes through education/ information	residents have a say	residents directly involved
5. Residential location	solar orientation	arbitrary orientation	optional use of PSE	use of Active Solar Energy (ASE)	dwelling type determined by orientation
	PSE/ASE/PV		80% between SE & SW; panel angle ASE/PV 20°-50°	90% between SSE & SSW; panel angle ASE/PV 20°-50°	100% South; ASE / PV 20°- 50°
	obstruction angle 30°	obstruction angle 24° (1:2.2)	obstruction angle, 17° (1:3.2)	obstruction angle, 14° (1:4)	

#	Topic	D	C	B	A
	noise	Noise Abatement Act with exemption(s)	Noise Abatement Act without exemption	quiet facade (front) for every dwelling	natural background
6. Waste	from construction	to waste disposal or land-fill	sorted/separated removal	use for landscaping public areas	everything returns to recycle process
6.2	organic	to waste disposal or land-fill	sorted/separated removal	choice of compost for own use or collection	compost within the neighbourhood
6.3	glass	in glass recycle bin	glass recycle bin 60 metres from dwelling	collect in crates at home	deposit system
6.4	paper	sporadic collection	paper recycle bin in neighbourhood	collected from home at predetermined times	recycling 100%
6.5	chemical	chemical collection truck	collected separately	depot in neighbouhood; open 60 hours /week	does not exist
6.6	large waste	incinerated or to land-fill	special days for recycling (tempor. local covered storage)	second hand use; service area in neighbourhood	repair in the neighbourhood
6.7	dog poop	not permitted on footpath	dog walking route, dog toilet	cleaned-up by dog owner	no dogs in the city
7. Traffic	The further the better	The car can do without you for a day.		No place like home.	only method of transportation
7.1	slow traffic	inferior; detours	defined structure	right-of-way	optimally organised
7.2	public transport	bus in the neighbourhood	bus stop max. 500 metres, 2 per hour	fast public transp. at max. dist. of 300 m, 4 per hour	car-free neighb., shared car ownership
7.3	car traffic	the car is sacred	narrower traffic lanes	subordinate; no right-of-way	
7.4	parking	at front door: parking standard 1.5	park at end of street, parking standard 1.0; teleworking	differentiated parking plan, parking standard 0.5	parking at entrance to neighb./standard 0.25
8. Pipes/cables	route	spread throughout the street	concentrated in narrow strips	connected to foundations	prevent necessity of pipes/cables
8.2	material	PVC/copper	ceramics/concrete/PE/steel	limited diameter	
9. Building material	choice based on investment				
9.1	pavement	asphalt	concrete/brick paving or tiles	half-paved, limited paved surfaces	rubble, wood chips, etc.
9.2	benches/lights/etc.	galvan. metal, alumin, tropical hardw.	brick, spar	European hard wood, recycled plastics, steel	loam, vegetation, etc.

Method of four variants: DCBA

Good designers always see more, sometimes even many, possibilities or variations. Other disciplines do not always have a clear overview of this abundance of ideas. Grouping the variants into environmental themes and arranging them according to environmental goals will provide a convenient method for all concerned.

Possible themes include: energy, building materials, water, food and waste. The four levels can be classified in ascending order of environmental friendliness.
D: The normal situation;
C: Correct normal use;
B: Minimizing damage to the environment;
A: Autonomous; the ideal situation.

This method is used throughout this book to clarify the possible options at the different levels.
Having considered all these variants and their impact on the design, costs, and in terms of required skills, etc., the level of ambition of the project can be selected. Once this level has been chosen (after discussing possible conflicts between areas like energy, water, materials, etc.), the urban design phase can start. Here again, the situation is complex. How can the different levels of ambition and wishes be integrated to create a sound and sustainable area?

DCBA Chart: Urban design
© BOOM, Environmental Research & Design Office, Oude Delft 49, Delft

A method used on several places in the Netherlands, which has proven to be very useful and in which there is growing interest in the US, is the 'Maximization Method'.

Maximization Method for sustainable urban design

The Maximization Method is a design method for urban design projects which clarifies the structuring influence of environmental and other themes in the design process.

Site analyses

Design processes are often carried out in a highly individual way, which makes it difficult to find out exactly how they were arrived at after the fact. The process, from the site analysis and schedule of requirements through to the design itself, takes place largely inside the head of the designer or designers. Sometimes the concept appears 'out of the blue' and even the other disciplines directly involved don't know exactly why this concept was chosen as the best.

The Maximization Method makes it possible:
• to work in an interdisciplinary way;
• to make clear what the structuring themes are and which themes have priority;
• to clarify the design process;
• to achieve a better result.

First, we have to define the structuring themes. From an environmental viewpoint these will be such things as energy, water, landscape, nature, soil, and traffic, together with restrictive themes like air pollution, soil pollution and traffic noise. Other themes are also possible, such as archaeology and, of course, existing housing areas, schools and the community as well as shopping centres.

The Maximization Method: the design process time-line. *Source: Kees Duijvestein*

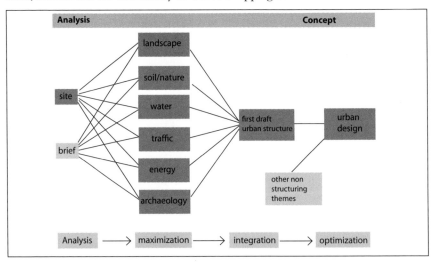

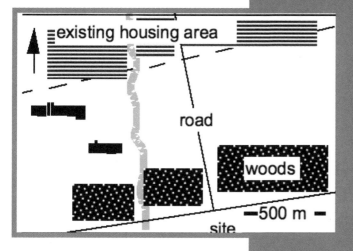

The method (example)

The site and the brief

Let us take a site in the southern part of the Netherlands. The site is about 1500 metres long and 500 metres wide. There is a railway line on the North side, the site is crossed by a small river and a road, there are woods on the South side and behind the woods there is another road that leads towards the city centre. The soil is mostly sandy with a clay/ sand mixture near to the river. The brief/schedule of requirements is to build 2000 houses, schools and a small centre. No more than 25% of the houses may be medium/high rise, up to 10 storeys.

Maximizations

Now we are going to add the 'maximizations' Maximizations are drawings of urban structures, drawn on as if only one theme (e.g., landscape) and environmental quality are important. Forget for a moment all the other themes! This is done for all the chosen themes. The drawings can be made in subgroups with the disciplines involved for that theme.

Landscape

The landscape maximization shows the possibility of building almost everywhere between the woods and the railway line, the area along the river is very nice and can be left open.

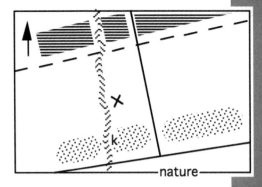

—nature—

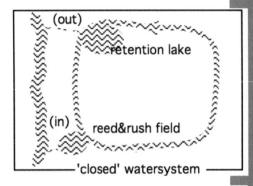

'closed' watersystem

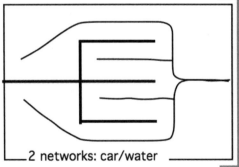

2 networks: car/water

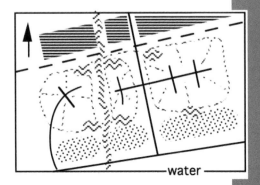

—water—

Nature

The nature maximization marks with an X a special biotope of a protected salamander species and some orchids (e.g., orchis palustris) The k indicates the nest of a kingfisher.

Water

For the water maximization we use the principle of the closed water system and the two networks strategy (water and infrastructure).

A *closed water system* enables us to keep clean water and rainwater inside the system and relatively dirty agricultural water out. Therefore a fluctuation in the water level has to be permitted. The highest level, after a rainy period, is 40 cm higher than the lowest level after a dry period.

If the level gets higher, water will be let out, if the level is lower, water from the river will be let in through a field of water and riverbank plants, like reed and rush, to purify the water. There is a retention lake for extra surface water to keep water in.

The *strategy of the two networks* is used to organise the urban layout in such a way that polluting motorised traffic is kept away from the water system as much as possible. The water system conducts the rainwater to the surface water; only the rainwater that falls on heavy traffic roads goes to the sewage system.

These principles are then combined for the maximization. An extra lake is planned near the woods to infiltrate water for the trees.

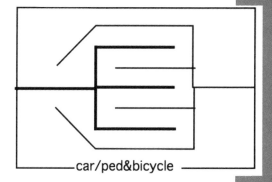

car/ped&bicycle

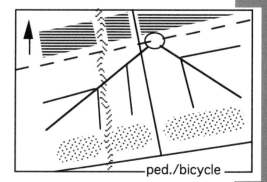

ped./bicycle

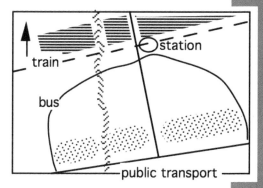

train

bus

public transport

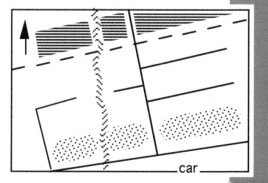

car

Traffic

For the traffic maximization we make a distinction between non-motorised traffic like pedestrians and bicycles, public transport, like buses and trains and other motorised traffic, like cars. We try to keep these systems apart to make it safer for people.

For pedestrians and cyclists we organise the shortest route to the planned centre and railway station.

For the public transport we organise an extra railway station and lead the existing bus to the city, through the neighbourhood to the station.

The road system for cars will be connected to the existing road network; there is no car connection over the river.

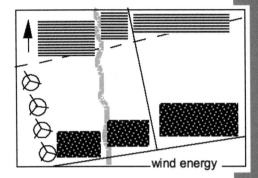

wind energy

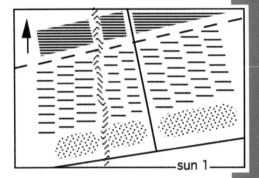

sun 1

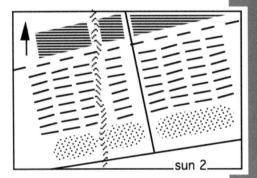

sun 2

Energy

For energy we will look at how renewable energy, like solar energy and wind energy, can be used.

Since the prevailing wind in the Netherlands comes from the South West and the landscape is open in that direction, wind generators can be placed there.

To use solar energy the best orientation for the façades of the houses is South. Therefore the building blocks should be East-West. In the figure Sun 1, passive solar energy (direct gain through the windows) allows for a variation of 20 degrees; active solar energy (photovoltaic cells for electricity and solar collectors for warm water) allows for a variation of 40 degrees.

A bigger variation reduces the energetic return by too much. The long lines on the site, like the railway line and edge of the woods, have a 12 degree variation from East-West; the building blocks can therefore be better placed in relation to the landscape elements (see figure "sun 2").

Archaeology

Urban design is not only structured by environmental themes. Other considerations like existing housing areas and shopping centres or entirely different disciplines like archaeology, for instance, can impose restrictions but also offer opportunities. In our area there is a prehistoric site dating from the Iron Age (1800 BC) about 1 metre below ground level. The specialists want to save it for later generations, so it is

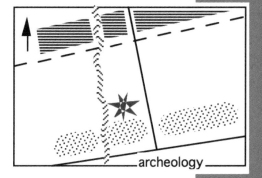

archeology

not permitted to build on it but planting trees is also not good for conservation as the roots could demolish the prehistoric site. A green area with playing fields may offer a solution.

Combination of the maximizations

The first draft urban structure/design shows a possible combination of the maximizations. Starting from the left, there are three urban villas 10 storeys high and three wind generators, each 40 metres high. Along the railway line there are building blocks six storeys high, on a base of a two-storey high building. The whole structure is a combination of housing and offices and other businesses. It protects the other houses from the noise of the railway. There is a new railway station building on both sides of the track. All the houses are oriented to the South - South-East to gain as much solar energy as possible. West of the river and in the eastern part there is a closed water system, in the central area the rain is immediately infiltrated or it flows directly to the river. The bus passes by the station, the northern bridge over the river is only for the bus and non-motorised traffic. The other bridge is for pedestrians and cyclists and is part of a direct route to the station.

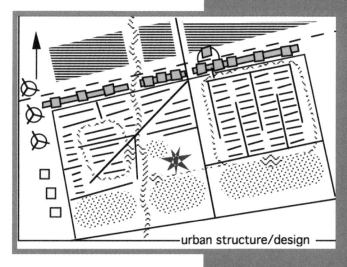

urban structure/design

CASE STUDY

Nieuwland

Nieuwland is divided into 4 quadrants. The water system is an integral part of the development. A large proportion of the houses face south, and use solar energy for hot water, heating or electricity. The water quadrant, upper right corner, was fully developed towards maximum solar energy use, and is main part of the 1 MW solar demo project.

Nieuwland was the first project to upscale sustainable Building to a very large neighbourhood, with urban design as a guiding basis for the houses. Environmental quality, residents perspectives and quality in planning where guiding, without excessive extra costs.

The plan had supervisors, that operated above developers and architects. (see table DCBA)

• Social Quality:
  (People) C/B
• Environmental Quality:
  (Planet) C
• Economic Quality:
  (Profit) C
• Design Quality:
  (Project) B ■

Nieuwland Urban Plan and Project 'Energy balance houses', Solar hot water and electricity generation in an integrated roof, Amersfoort.
Source: Ronald Rovers

Project and Process management

For a long time, buildings in the Netherlands were constructed one by one, creating an organic growth over time in urban neighbourhoods. After the Second World War, when large numbers of houses had to be built and reconstructed, and with the rise of industrial production techniques, the planning and construction of groups of houses became general practice, sometimes thousands of the same kind on a rigid grid. In the 1980s it was recognised that in order to develop attractive and human scale neighbourhoods, a more sophisticated design process was needed, and architects started experimenting with all the elements of a neighbourhood (e.g., ponds, road plans, varied types of housing, etc.). It was not until the early 1990s that it was recognised that a sustainable view of neighbourhood development could offer a good guiding principle for the design of housing areas. In the Netherlands a first attempt was made with *Ecolonia*, a demonstration project. Ecolonia's primary purpose was to give an impetus to sustainable building in mainstream Dutch residential building. The project also created an opportunity to gain experience with the development of a sustainable housing project.

In the Netherlands there was already plenty of expertise in the fields of energy conservation, sustainable energy and construction, but expertise in life-cycle management and quality improvement was fragmented and certainly not widely available. The lessons learned were mainly related to the process, the way in which the various parties worked together on the project. An interdisciplinary approach with developer, architects and experts contributed to the success of the project.

In the years that followed, the lessons learned were tested in several projects and led to modifications and guidelines being drawn up for housing developments. Official packages of measures and approaches were published for residential and non-residential buildings. Attention was given to the possibilities of energy infrastructure, water in the environment, south orientation, indoor climate and environment, traffic and car parking, as well as the contribution and participation of future residents. Many of these projects and experiences were published in periodicals and publications. An overview of some of them can be found in the publication 'Framework for the Future' and in the publication 'Opting for Change'.

The ideas developed came together in a recent important project on sustainable housing: *EVA Lanxmeer* in Culemborg. It was privately initiated by the E.V.A. Foundation, and the project was developed and realised in cooperation with the municipality of Culemborg. The first dwellings were handed over in 2000.

In this project the knowledge gained from Ecolonia and beyond was incorporated in an integrated approach based on technological, economic, ecological and social-cultural development. The conditions for sustainable development have to be consciously designed into the urban plan, which requires interdisciplinary

Ecolonia
Source: Ger de Vries

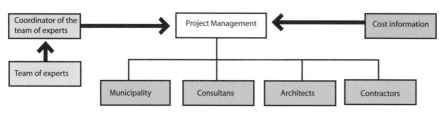

Ecolonia project:
simplified diagram of
organisation.
Source: Ger de Vries

Ecolonia
Source: Ger de Vries

cooperation between the various parties in the design, planning and building process.

The plan is based on a co-production with future residents and users and consists of:
- 250 single family houses and apartments;
- ecological offices, workshops and studios;
- integral water system with biological water purification integrated in landscape architecture;
- energy concept based on renewable energy;
- ecological city farm for local food production;
- ecological conference and education centre.

To think in concepts creates more freedom for design. Both projects were based on a concept and a programme of requirements. Both projects have shown that it is important to create a coordinated interdisciplinary approach among the various partners involved in the process at their own level of detail. And everybody needs to be involved at a very early stage of the process. With this kind of innovative project it is actually necessary to operate as a building team.

Process organisation

The optimisation of the project process is best illustrated by comparing the two examples, the Ecolonia project completed in 1992 and EVA Lanxmeer now partly completed and partly still under construction. Evaluation of the organisation of the Ecolonia and EVA Lanxmeer projects shows similarities and differences. Ecolonia was developed by a contractor. A major part of EVA Lanxmeer was developed by the municipality up to the design phase.

Ecolonia was organised along two lines: firstly, by the developer who maintained contacts with the municipality, consultants, architects and contractors, which is the 'normal' procedure in the Netherlands. The second line consisted of experts who transferred their knowledge to the developer and especially the architects in the design process. At first the experts participated in the discussions with the architect and the developer. However, this did not appear to be practical. As the process progressed, it was necessary to limit the number of experts in the discussions to one or two or just the coordinator of the expert team. Specific questions were raised and discussed with the relevant experts on that topic. During the process there was direct contact between the developer or architect and the experts. The experts also handled the monitoring programme. The coordination of the experts had a positive effect on the integration of their advice, its application in the Ecolonia project and the evaluation of the monitoring programme.

EVA Lanxmeer: urban
development plan.
Source:
Joachim Eble Architektur,
Tübingen (Duitsland) and
Copijn Utrecht Tuin- en
landschapsarchitecten bv,
Utrecht.

Project team EVA Lanxmeer
Municipality, EVA Found., project manager BEL (future
residents), BCW (housing association) and one or more
coordinators of the projects when required.

Coordination group
Project manager, municipality, EVA Found., project
coordinators, BEL (future residents)

Projects
- project 1
- project 2
- etc.

Areas
- urban planning
- energy plan
- water system
- etc.

Design group
Project managers, municipality, EVA Found., urban
design, landscape design and architects

EVA Lanxmeer: simplified
diagram of organisation.
Source; Ger de Vries

In the EVA Lanxmeer project a rather different policy was adopted. The process centred around the involvement of a large number of participants in a project team. This team consisted of representatives of the Municipality of Culemborg and the E.V.A. Foundation together with the urban planner, two representatives of the future residents and an investment expert. Other experts were invited as and when needed. An external project manager with a general knowledge of and an interest in environmental design was appointed. The project manager brought the necessary expertise into the process, if necessary, after consulting experts or invited experts in the project team. The project team also checked the plan and the results of the design group in relation to the basic concept and the programme of requirements. The municipality's traditional contribution of local services and facilities was handled by the coordination group, which included representatives of the project team.

A missing link in this process was a joint discussion between the urban planner, landscape designer and all the architects of the site. Another critical factor was that the municipality developed some of the housing right up to the final design. The knowledge of the project developer / contractor could not be used in the design phase. The project developer / contractor was now only an executing party. The building contractor's advice was set aside. When problems occurred later due to deficiencies in dwellings a dispute arose about the question of responsibility.

In Ecolonia the architects had to deal with too many experts. This was recognised later in the design process when more bilateral consultation took place. In the EVA Lanxmeer project there was insufficient communication and exchange of information between the architects and the experts and among the architects themselves. In both projects the cost estimation aspect was a problem, which was identified too late.

The Ecolonia organisation actually worked very well. But don't ask architects to deal with a surfeit of experts. Someone to coordinate the experts and one or two experts, if necessary, is sufficient to ensure that the experts' wishes and recommendations are taken into account at the start of the design process. The design group for EVA Lanxmeer worked very well, but more attention needed to be given to communication between the urban planner, landscape designer and all the architects of the site: at some point in the process they should get together to discuss common issues. A cost estimator also has to be brought in at an early stage of the design process.

Design Process*

Compared to a conventional design approach, the integrated design process is characterised by the integration of activities in a project team. This implies that several disciplines (client, architect, project manager, consultants in the fields of environment, urban planning, landscape, energy, water, etc.) are involved in the design process right from the outset, or even before that, when the brief is drawn up.

The integrated design process itself typically consists of a number of design loops resulting in products that provide milestones. These milestones function as decision documents at transition moments in the design process, as it moves from one phase to the next. Experience has been gained with this process from different demonstration projects.

A common understanding of the client's needs and expectations is a necessary pre-requisite for an integrated design process and could even be considered as a preliminary design loop. Understanding the design task means not only studying the brief (programme of requirements) but also discussing it together with the client and assimilating and noting the client's expectations.

The structure of the process

The first design loop starts before the actual design activities begin. The design process starts with informal discussions and a kick-off workshop in the startup and preparation phase. This approach can be seen as a first design loop in the sense that the purpose is to achieve a clear understanding of the design task. Even the client sometimes redefines his needs based on the discussions in the kick-off workshop, which makes it an important step towards realising a satisfactory end product.

In general, the design loops consist of a mix of activities. The main activities within a design loop involve multidisciplinary working sessions in which design options are discussed and judged related to the overall performance of the site and the buildings. Dependencies between different subsystems of the building are addressed and through trade-off analyses, the team makes design decisions to avoid sub-optimisation. All sorts of individual or bilateral work has to be done to prepare for or follow up these working sessions.

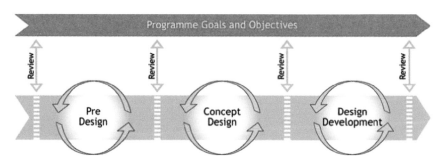

Design loop with feedback *

Integration is a very important issue especially in the early stages of the design process and adding a facilitator to the team is recommended if the team is not familiar with an integrated design process. The facilitator has to know the wishes and recommendations of the experts in the different fields and has to bring these into the design process. Eventually some experts can be invited to take part in the design process. In the final stages of the design phase the process takes on a more conventional character. Where the design includes innovative technologies, integration continues to be an important issue right up to the construction and exploitation phases. The early stages of the design process may subsequently be a little more time-consuming and costly, but a more consistent and integrated pre-design prevents inefficiencies at later stages of the design process and results in a better cost-performance ratio of the building.

Stakeholder role*

Demonstration projects have shown that an integrated design process is not a rigid approach and can be applied in a wide range of projects. Crucial to an integrated design process is a competent design team and a clear design task. This can easily be understood as a trivial statement but the fact that dealing with an integrated design process and not a traditional design process makes the difference. The integrated design process imposes special requirements on the team and the description of the design task that are not self-evident.

It is important that the actors of the design team have an open attitude towards integration and are truly willing to participate in an integrated design process. The clients' needs (i.e. brief, programme of requirements) must also facilitate an integrated approach. This requires a clear concept and a clear but not unnecessarily detailed description and a possibility to accept modifications that lead to a more optimal end result. How the role of the various actors in the integrated design process is structured, as well as the individual competences and motivation of the actors is crucial to a successful integrated design process. All of these aspects played an important role in the demonstration projects.

The client

The idea to start an integrated design process almost never comes from the client. In most cases the architect, consultants or experts take the initiative. In many cases the client has to be introduced into the integrated design process and the advantages and risks have to be discussed. If the client has a clear understanding of the approach and chooses to follow this path, the next important step is to discuss and agree on the basic conditions required for a successful process. If the client's intentions are not clear from the outset, the process will be adversely affected. A motivated and actively involved client is very important.

* Adapted form: The Integrated Design Process in Practice: demonstration projects evaluated.

The team

For a successful design the whole team has to have a positive attitude towards an integrated design process. To establish this, at least one motivated and enthusiastic person is needed to act as the driving force during the design process and where innovative technologies are involved, during the realisation phase too. The design team and the client in particular must have confidence in this person.

The future

An integrated approach will become common in the Netherlands in the design of residential and non-residential buildings. When the economic climate is not so good, short term solutions are favoured, but since the 1980s there has been a trend towards a more integrated design process. In complex situations, such as the retrofitting of neighbourhoods, it is essential to adopt an approach which also incorporates social, economic and environmental factors. Over the last decade the Dutch government had adopted the integrated design process has for its non-residential building projects. Today integrated design is becoming increasingly prevalent in semi-experimental settings. The bioclimatic design approach focuses on the possibilities of the site and the environment but often follows an integrated design process taking into account the wishes of future tenants and owners in the interests of helping to create a sustainable environment.

Building design

The history of green building design in the Netherlands goes back to the early 1990s when the Dutch government drew up a green paper with targets for the transport, building and construction industries. Covenants were made for all parties in the industry. To underpin these covenants discussions were held in different fora. The main outcome was an awareness of the impact of urban planning, architecture and construction on the environment. The main measures in the building sector were: water and energy savings, collection and recycling of waste and an awareness of the environment by the population. As a result, many laws were changed and the building regulations have a chapter on environmental impact, risk and health. These have influenced design a lot.

To the untrained observer there will not be much difference between houses designed today and 15 years ago, all the changes that have taken

Façade with shading
Source:
BEAR Architecten

place will not be obvious. A house is still essentially a brick building, with windows and doors, and a flat or sloping roof. The differences, however, are in many of the details inside and outside the house. Energy was the main reason for most of the changes, although lately we see the influence of new materials concepts as well. The main construction, seen in the cross-section drawings and construction details, underwent the most drastic changes; the inside and outside walls have been completely disconnected, thereby avoiding cold bridges and air leakage, resulting in completely new details.

A second area of change was the interior: living rooms are more related to the outdoor space or garden, rooms were placed in relation to their function during the day or night, requiring sun radiation and daylight or not, leading to optimum use of sunshine and daylight. This, of course, is closely related to the choice of window size, which in turn is also influenced by the level of passive solar energy used in the energy concept for the house.

A purely passive solar energy concept leads to a different design than a design that relies more on energy-efficient installation concepts. It is expected that passive concepts will take the lead, however, as this approach combines sustainable design with comfortable living without major extra investments. Therefore large windows facing South and small windows facing North, overhangs and shading devices, will influence the architecture. Blinds can be fitted to control overheating, with overhangs to protect the façade and reduce maintenance. The building construction has changed as well: the span of the house can now be made 6 to 7 metres wide without any bearing walls anymore. This introduces flexibility in lay out and possible changes in use over the lifetime of the house: This should make it more attractive to use the house for a longer period of time and to adapt it to different lifestyles (thus avoiding demolition). Interior walls are increasingly designed for re-use if removed. The minimum ceiling height has been raised by law from 2.40 to 2.60 metres (as it was 100 years ago), as research has shown that the extra materials input is offset by greater flexibility in the future, e.g. to integrate new installation concepts, avoid waste in renovation or to prevent early demolition. Door heights have also been increased, mainly because Dutch people are getting taller. In many cases, kitchens are not installed as standard, since it has been shown that Dutch people generally prefer to have their own choice of kitchen and do not use the standard kitchen, thereby spoiling materials and creating a lot of unnecessary waste.

Another important interior change is in the heating concept: 15 years ago a central heating system with radiators below every window was the standard. Since the insulation values of glazing has improved a lot (low- E glazing with U ≤ 1.3 s.i.) cold downdraughts along windows is no longer a decisive factor, and as new glass technologies have become more energy efficient *and* comfortable, floor heating has become more usual. This gives more freedom in terms of the interior decoration. Another more visible change is to be seen in the growing use of active solar systems, such as solar hot water collectors and photovoltaic electricity panels on roofs (and façades), sometimes visible as panels between the tiles but also well integrated as tiles or roof tops. The latest building-integrated trends are small wind energy devices for flat and sloping roofs.

Process

A design process starts with the brief, the location and the influence of the surroundings and culture on that location. The brief will give us the information about the space we need, the comfort level we require, the budget we have, and the energy that we will use. The surroundings will give us a specific climate and specific resources. Every site has many potential resources, like nature, the landscape and the climate: sun, wind, rain and earth, can all be helpful. If we can use the local climate and local resources, this will reduce the pressure on the environment. This provides the starting point for the design process which brings together and materialises all the topics discussed in the foregoing chapters. This is generally called the 'bio-climatic approach' or 'climatic design'.

- Applying the principles of bio-climatic design is the first step towards sustainable design. The main objective of climatic design is to provide 'comfortable' living conditions with a minimum and meaningful input of non-sustainable energy. This reduces investment and running costs (energy), as well as environmental damage.

- The second step is to reduce the environmental impact of the building. This is done by studying the flow of energy, water and materials that go through a building during its construction and lifetime. A strategy to achieve this is called 'The three step approach' or *Trias Ecologica*. The steps are:
1. Reduce the use of resources (energy, water, materials);
2. Use renewable resources (solar energy, renewables);
3. Optimize non-renewables (re-use of waste).

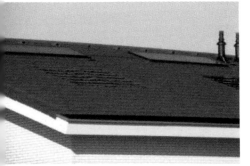

Lafarge roof with PV and ridge collector. *Source: BEAR Architecten*

- The third step is 'human comfort'. This is not just thermal comfort but also emotional comfort. Thermal comfort depends on issues like temperature, humidity, air movement and radiation. Emotional comfort deals with the interaction between people and buildings. How can a user influence the building or his working space? This human factor is very important to successful sustainable building design. Research has shown that users who are not involved in the design of a new building will have many more complaints about their working or living space than users that are involved in the design process.

Sustainable design principle

Design process in steps

1. Requirements (brief) for each building/urban plan;

2. Information about the climate; local energy and water consumption;

3. Information about the local culture and building methods;

4. Requirements for the comfort level that is needed;

5. Available energy sources and expected energy consumption;

6. Conceptual design for the building (based on the local climate).

The design process is important to make sure that the right decisions are made at the right time. This can save money. It is important to combine different measures in such a way that the total investment will be less than the total sum of the individual measures. An example of this is the use of solar systems as shading systems: the total investment will be much less than investing separately in a shading system and a solar system. Besides this, the output will be much higher and so will the return on investment. The solar system will produce energy and this energy will not reach the interior of the building. So there will also be less need for cooling. To achieve this it is necessary to start thinking about the total environmental building design during the preliminary design phase. At this stage, thinking about materials should be about considering the possibility of refurbishing an existing building instead of building a new one. And thinking about how to use existing materials instead of new materials. Is it possible to build a building that can easily be transformed for other functions or that can be easily disassembled for future usage?

The location and the orientation of the building are very important for the integration of all forms of renewable energy sources. The correct orientation of the building will provide it with sunshine and protection against cold winds in winter and with shading and a cool breeze in summer. Naturally, the immediate surroundings and the landscaping will influence the amount of sun and daylight, wind and humidity around a building. An urban situation with only concrete pavements is the worst possible situation for the surrounding climate. An open, nicely landscaped situation with trees is the opposite. In many cases there are not very many choices. The surroundings are there and cannot be influenced by the client or the architect. In which event it will be up to the creativity of the architect to use ponds, basins, green façades and green roofs to improve the surroundings.

The organisation of the plan has a direct relationship with the orientation. Living and working spaces that are mainly used in the morning or the day should be located on the East and South sides. Spaces that don't need much heating or do not require much thermal comfort should be orientated on the West side. Spaces with equipment that produces a lot of heat (e.g. kitchens and computer workspaces) should be on the North side. Spaces with a high indoor temperature demand throughout the year (like a bathroom) should be put in a central place inside the house. Cooler spaces (like storage) should be on the outer cooler side of the house. Buffer space that does not require a stable indoor temperature is useful between the indoor and the outdoor climate. All these design decisions have to be taken very carefully. Sometimes it will not be possible to incorporate a certain decision, because there are other requirements like daylight or noise control, that limit the design possibilities.

Main aspects

The main sustainable aspects will now be considered in more depth in the following brief overview.

Materials

Applying the three-step strategy to materials at building design level means asking yourself:

a. Can I reduce the quantity of materials?

b. Can I use renewable materials? and,

c. Can I optimize the use of non-renewable materials or use materials with the lowest environmental impact?

The steps described above are just the start in reducing the amount of materials used. At building level it could be minimizing construction details. This is a matter of creative thinking and trends. A pure design does not need much decoration. However, not all clients will be convinced of this.

The range of renewable materials is vast. Local resources are the first to be used. There is an important future role for alternatives from agricultural crops and waste, as well as for Bamboo. Bamboo is not only a low-tech material but it can be used as a high-tech material as well. There is a lot of research being carried out on the application of bamboo for plywood, flooring and I-beams. The use of these materials means that design-related choices have to be made very early in the design process.

Water

There is a growing demand for fresh water. Actually, water in buildings is mainly used as a transport medium: to transport heat in a heating system, to transport waste in a sewage system and to transport dirt while cleaning the building. Less than 10% of the demand for water is for direct human use, like drinking or cooking. Many functions can be done with less water or with water with a lower level of quality, like rainwater or treated grey water. For the design process, it is important to take decisions about the amount of water that can be buffered in or around the

Bamboo plywood, laminated bamboo I-beams and bamboo culms knot
Source: INBAR Beijing

buildings, the possibility of having a water tank, the space for installations and the distances between installation and taps. This will also have an impact on the hot water system. Long piping will involve more use of energy and water.

Energy

Here the focus is on conservation, renewables and efficient non-renewables. The main issues in building design are solar energy (heating), ventilation (cooling), shading and daylight.

Solar energy

The design is based on the direct use of solar energy (passive solar energy). Because of the change in use and the desire to heat rooms at night (after sunset), this passive principle is extended with active solar systems. A rule for the cooler seasons is to maximize heat gain during the day and minimize heat loss. This means that buildings have to face South and Southeast to receive solar energy through the windows, especially in the morning hours. This approach is based on traditional Chinese wisdom, and some new techniques can provide an interesting addition to this. For hot water there are roof-integrated solar thermal panels. Solar thermal systems can be connected for short-term storage, allowing the solar heat gained during the day used in the evening and on cloudy days. There is no need to store solar energy for a long time. In general, we will use electricity from the grid, although photovoltaic (PV) modules can be used to generate electricity as well. The application of PV modules is a growing market that started in Japan about ten years ago. Today, the Chinese industry is entering this market too. PV modules on the roof can serve a double function: as façade cladding and a shading system. Integration of the systems in buildings (BIPV) has to be done at an early stage in the design process.

Shading

Summer is the period with the highest electrical energy demand. This is mainly because of cooling. The heat load of buildings can be decreased with the right measures in the building skin and through the applications in the building. Step one is to avoid excessive heat load from applications in working or living spaces. Monitors, televisions and refrigerators produce a lot of heat. Energy efficient appliances like flat screens are a much better solution. Step two is to avoid solar energy getting into the building in summer. This is a matter of designing the right façade and installing sun blinds. A building with overhangs will be more comfortable in summer.

Ventilation

Ventilation has to be controlled in the building, especially in kitchens and bathrooms. The entrance has to be protected against draughts by an entrance porch.

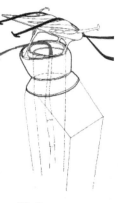

Windtower
Source: WindTowers, Battle McCarthy Consulting Engineers. 1999.

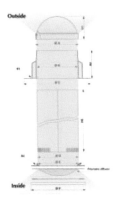

Daylight tube
*Source: Monolight
brochure*

For the warm seasons, it is important to minimize heat gain during the day and enable heat loss at night. Even when the average temperature is not very high, strong sunlight can heat up buildings. Indoor temperatures above 22°C (approx. 74°F) are less comfortable, but with good natural ventilation the heat load can be lowered. The thermal mass of the building is also suitable for storing heat by day in the construction and releasing heat at night when the building is ventilated with cooler air.

In an energy-efficient building, ventilation has to be controlled. This means that there is almost no unwanted and uncontrolled air circulation. Windows and doors do not permit air movement when they are closed. To ensure that there is enough fresh air, especially for smokers in a building, we need to calculate the amount of air and the openings for the air. However, to keep air moving, we need a mechanical system (with ventilator). This type of system is more energy efficient because it will provide more ventilation where it is needed and less where it is not. The next step is a ventilation system with heat recovery. This system has inlets to introduce fresh air into rooms and outlets to remove polluted air from other rooms. Both air streams cross, and the heat from the vented air is used to heat the fresh air. The efficiency of a heat exchanger may be between 60-90%. The availability of installations will determine the final system selected.

L + M:
Greenhouse and facade
with shading
*Source:
BEAR Architecten*

R:
DKA visitorcentre
source: Ronald Rovers

Daylight

No matter how good the day lighting design is, virtually every building needs an artificial lighting system as well – for night time use, for windowless spaces, or to supplement daylight when it falls below acceptable levels. The requirements for light (daylight and artificial light) are that it be functional, comfortable and energy saving. Functional light means enough light for the work that has to be done, comfortable

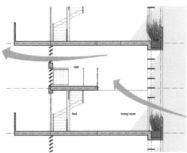

Cross-section of an
apartment with daylight
and ventilation.
Source:
BEAR Architecten

light means that the difference in light levels in a room is not more than
1 to 3; glare is also an important issue, as large windows have to be
covered to prevent glare. Energy-saving light means reducing the number
of hours that artificial light is used and, if artificial light is used, it is
provided by energy-efficient tubes and bulbs.

If a day lighting system is to result in energy savings, it is important
that artificial lighting is not switched on as long as daylight provides
adequate illumination. This can be achieved by providing light switches
close to (not too large) zones of light parallel to the façade. Simple local
switching of this kind can produce 20% energy savings. Simple automatic control
systems with timers and/or sensors can also produce significant energy savings.
Light tubes can be used in buildings to bring daylight deep into the heart of the
building without extending the heat load in summer.

The climatic design strategy can be used in single-family dwellings, houses,
apartments, and all types of commercial buildings. For apartments a void may be
ideal to create natural ventilation inside. A green façade will have a positive impact
on the heat-island effect. Daylight is important, but at the same time, good shading
may be more important for comfortable indoor temperatures in the summer.

DCBA Targets

D: meeting legal requirements
C: Energy-efficient design, best practice measures and products used
B: Conceptual, bioclimat design, optimised materials used
A: Zero-energy design, only renewable materials used, flexible, demountable

GENERAL MEASURES

Heating (winter)	Ventilation (winter)	Daylight	Rainwater	
1. High thermal insulation	1. Controlled ventilation and heat recovery	1. Direct daylight	1. Make green roofs and façades to	3. Keep mechanical equipment together
2. Protection against wind	**Cooling (summer)**	2. Void in house	collect rainwater	**Materials**
3. Use of direct passive solar energy	1. Outside shading	3. Light tube	2. Collect grey water for toilet flush	1. Use less material (ceramic tiles instead
4. Use of thermal solar energy with storage	2. Internal airflow	**Electricity**	3. Treat water with plants	of bricks)
	3. Thermal mass	1. Switch off stand-by power		2. Use renewable material (bamboo
	4. Day-night ventilation	2. Light sensors (daylight, movement, time)	**Water**	plywood and flooring)
5. Auxiliary heating with best available sources	5. Green + water	3. Building integration of photovoltaic panels	1. Use water saving taps and shower	3. Use local material (concrete without
	Hot water		2. Use water saving toilets	steel, natural stone)
	1. Solar thermal energy			

CASE STUDIES

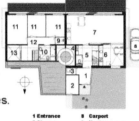

255 CO₂ neutral houses Lelystad-South NL

Winning design (BEAR Architecten Gouda NL) of an international competition. The purpose was to design 255 houses
with the optimum CO_2 neutral energy system for these houses.
Selection was made upon the urban and architecture design
and the energy concept for these houses. One of the design
issues was to design 'modern' farms that meet the energy
demands. The whole area is known as a recreative living area.

1 Entrance	8 Carport
2 Storage	9 Heatrecovery
3 Heat pump	10 Bathroom
4 Watertank	11 Bedroom
5 Hall	12 Hall/stairs
6 Kitchen	13 Vide
7 Living room	14 Windmill

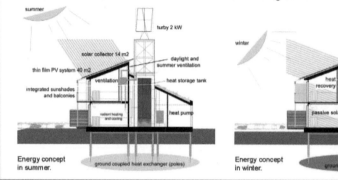

255 CO2 neutral
houses, Lelystad-
South (NL)
Source:
BEAR Architecten

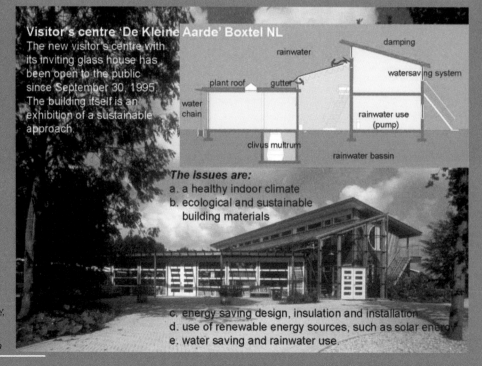

Visitor's centre 'De Kleine Aarde' Boxtel NL

The new visitor's centre with
its inviting glass house has
been open to the public
since September 30, 1995.
The building itself is an
exhibition of a sustainable
approach.

The issues are:
a. a healthy indoor climate
b. ecological and sustainable
   building materials
c. energy saving design, insulation and installation
d. use of renewable energy sources, such as solar energy
e. water saving and rainwater use.

Visitor's centre
'De Kleine Aarde',
Boxtel (NL)
Source:
BEAR Architecten

Epilogue

The knowledge and strategies described in this book represent the knowledge and experience of our leading experts on sustainable housing. Together, they have contributed to many successful projects in the Netherlands, in Europe and throughout the world. To implement this knowledge in daily practice, however, much more is needed. Tools have been developed to support the implementation in daily practice, for different stakeholders, and more are being developed, with many project developers and municipalities active in this field.

Unfortunately, governmental support for sustainable building in the Netherlands has decreased in recent years, and this body of knowledge – while firmly grounded in years of experience and with many successes – is currently not being applied to the fullest extent possible in the Netherlands. As environmental pressures on society increase, with rising oil prices, increasingly scarce land, increasing air pollution and so on, governmental support will most likely increase again. Furthermore, European Union rules and regulations are having a growing influence on national environmental policies. The Union is developing many new regulations and policies, which will force member countries to further improve their environmental performance.

Although the knowledge of sustainable building is now widely available in the Netherlands, still only a small part of new housing developments are designed and built in a truly sustainable way. While basic environmental performance has improved, it is still far away from the desired improvement of a factor 4 to 10, as will be needed to bring the Dutch housing stock within long-term sustainability limits. Assessments of finished projects indicate that the best projects have an environmental performance of approximately a factor 2 better than 10-15 years ago.

New housing *production* in the Netherlands is currently at a moderate level, due to lack of capacity in the building sector, the lack of available land, and changing zoning regulations. Since the Netherlands is a crowded country, there are many claims on land: not only for construction, but also for many other purposes, like the protection of breeding areas of rare species. Noise levels (from industry or transport) and air quality issues also limit the land usable for new housing developments. To cope with this situation, many ideas have been discussed and studied, like the pro-posed Pigcities (skyscrapers for pig farming, which would be both energy efficient and land saving), and cities of floating houses, capable of withstanding floods. Since the *Trias Ecologica* is a cornerstone of Dutch sustainable building philosophy (extensively used in this book), it can only be expected that the main focus in the future will be on existing buildings. The Dutch building stock, which is expected tobe the main component of housing until after 2050, has to be maintained, upgraded, extended and/or redeveloped to make existing homes fit for a sustainable future (with significantly lower fossil fuel consumption, strongly reduced materials consumption, as well as dramatically lower waste production, etc.). On a macro-economic level, Step 1 of the Trias Ecologica, to reduce the need for activities which affect the environment, also applies to the whole building stock: to reduce the need for newbuilding activity, by limiting the need for buildings or by re-using old buildings (with renovations, as needed).

Since the construction of a building has a major environmental impact (especially on land use, materials consumption, and waste production), reducing construction will lead to large reductions in the environmental pressure of the building sector (especially in countries with a large building stock, like the Netherlands). Of course, old buildings need to be refurbished to reduce the 'environmental running cost' involved in energy and water consumption. As was concluded in the Sustainable Technology Development programme (see description in the box on page 22), a factor 10 – or more – reduction in the environmental impact of the building and construction sector can only be achieved when the whole building stock is taken into account and is upgraded; logically, this requires that we focus on improving existing buildings.

The concepts presented here are valid both for new developments and for reuse of the existing housing stock. In fact, many new concepts that were originally developed for new buildings have been adapted to, and applied in, existing housing, asexperience has taught us that it is easier and cheaper to develop new solutions for new buildings first, when the designer has the maximum freedom and can fully control the design parameters.

Work is underway to further adapt the knowledge in this book to the future of 'building stock management', and this will continue to be an important issue for many years. The authors of this book are at the forefront of this development, both convinced of its importance and dedicated to its success. Updates of our progress and activities will be reported at the website www.sustainablebuilding.info.

Links and Bibliography

Bibliography

Anink, D. and C. Boonstra (1995) *Handbook of Sustainable Building: An environmental preference method for choosing materials in construction and renovation*, James & James, 176 pages

Battle McCarthy Consulting Engineers (1999) *Wind towers: Detail in building*, Wiley, 96 pages

Bitter C., J. van Ierland, A. Kruger, and C. Horch (1961) *Oordeel bewoners over bezonning van woningen (Residents' views of sunshine in dwellings)* TNO Instituut Gezondheidstechniek

Bottema, M. (1993) *Wind Climate and Urban Geometry*, PhD Thesis Eindhoven University of Technology

Brown, G. Z., and M. Dekay (2000) *Sun, Wind & Light: Architectural Design Strategies*, Wiley 400 pages

De Vries, G. (2004) *EVA-Lanxmeer te Culemborg Ervaringen met organisatie en proces*, V&L Consultants, Rotterdam, februari 2004.

Duurzaam en Gezond Bouwen (2004) (Healthy and sustainable building) Nibe Publishing bv, Bussem, the Netherlands

Duijvestein, K. (1997) *The environmental maximization method* In: Bekkering, H. et al., *The Architectural Annual 1995-1996*. Delft University of Technology / 010 Publishers

Duijvestein, K. (2002) *The environmental maximization method* In: De Jong, T.M. and D.J.M. Van der Voordt (eds) *Ways to study and research urban, architectural and technical design*, Delft University Press, 554 pages

Evaluatie Ecolonia – Eindrapportage (Evaluation Report) Novem, Sittard, 1994

Goed J. (2002) *EVA-Lanxmeer Culemborg: Beschrijving voorbeeldproject EVA-Lanxmeer op inhoud, proces en organisatie*, Goed Management & Advies, Culemborg, 26 april 2002

Hough, M. (1995) *Cities and natural process*, Routledge, 345 pages

Hyde, R. (2000) *Climate Responsive Design: A Study of Buildings in Moderate and Hot Humid Climates*, Spon, 256 pages

IEA Task 23 *Optimization of Solar Energy Use in Large Buildings*

Mels, A and G. Zeeman (2003) *Practical examples of DESAR concepts in urban areas in the Netherlands* In Proceedings 2nd symposium on Ecological Sanitation, Luebeck, Germany, April 2003.

Mels, A., K. Kujawa, J. Wilsenach, B. Palsma, G. Zeeman, and M. van Loosdrecht (2005) *Wastewater chain unchained: inventory of opportunities for more effi cient wastewater chain management by separated collection, treatment and reuse of flows* (in Dutch;). Dutch Foundation for Applied Water Research (STOWA).

Mels A., R. Otterpohl, and G. Zeeman (2005) *Paradigm shifts in wastewater management. Sustainable Building magazine. Rioned, 2003, Designing with rain water* (in Dutch). Rioned Foundation, Ede

O'Cofaigh, E., J.A. Olley, and J.O.Lewis (1996) *The Climatic Dwelling: An Introduction to Climate-Responsive Residential Architecture*, James and James, 165 pages

Olgyay, V. (1963) *Design with Climate: An approach to Bioclimatic Regionalism*, Princeton University Press

Poel, B., G. de Vries, and G. van der Cruchten (2002) *The Integrated Design Process in Practice: demonstration projects evaluated*, Consultants Arnhem, the Netherlands, June 03 2002.

Rutten, A.J.F. (2004) *A preliminary-design aid for daylight access to atrium or courtyard.* Proceedings of 21st International Conference PLEA, September 2004, p.1155-1157

SEV (2003) *Variantenboek milieuprestatie vormgegeven, (Variants made concrete in environmental performance)*, Aeneas, 100 pages

Sustainable Building: Frameworks for the Future (2000) SenterNovem, Utrecht, October 2000

The Road to Ecolonia: Evaluation and residents' survey (1995) SenterNovem, Utrecht, 1995

Toolkit Duurzame Woningbouwen (Sustainable building toolkit) (2005), SenterNovem Utrecht, 2005

Van Hal, A., G. de Vries, and J. Brouwers (2000) *Opting for change: Sustainable building in the Netherlands*, Aeneas, 136 pages

Van Lier, J.B., and G. Lettinga (1999) *Appropriate technologies for effective management of industrial and domestic wastewaters: the decentralised approach In Water, Science and Technology. 40 (7): 171-183.*

Wisse, J.A., and E. Willemsen (2003) *Standardization of wind comfort evaluation in the Netherlands, Proceedings of the 11th International Conference on Wind Engineering*, Lubbock, Texas, 2003.

Wisse, J.A., H.W. Krüs, and E. Willemsen (2002) *Wind comfort assessment by CFD, Proceedings of the symposium impact of wind and storm on city life and built environment*, CSTB, Nantes, June 2002.

Zeeman G., and G. Lettinga (1999) *The role of anaerobic digestion of domestic sewage in closing the water and nutrient cycle at community level In Water, Science and Technology, 39 (5): 187-194.*

Websites

This selection of websites can can also be found at:
www.sustainablebuilding.info (go to the Book section)

Database for projects and products
http://www.pvdatabase.com/search_form.cfm (In English)

Standardization, Norms and Codes
Building Decree
http://www.bouwbesluit-praktijk.nl (in Dutch)

NEN: Dutch Standardization Institute (in Dutch and in English)
http://www2.nen.nl/nen/servlet/dispatcher.Dispatcher?id=ABOUT_NEN

Centre for Civil Engineering Research and Codes
http://www.cur.nl (in Dutch and in English)

Policy and Research
Netherlands Ministry of Housing, Spatial Planning, and the Environment
http://www.vrom.nl (in Dutch)
http://www.vrom.nl/internationaal (in English)

Demonstration projects Industrial, Flexible and Demountable Construction, Programme of the Ministry of Economic Affairs, and the Ministry of Housing, Spatial Planning and the Environment
http://www.sev-realisatie.nl/lfd (in Dutch and in English)

World Health Organisation - Housing Issues
http://www.euro.who.int/Housing/Activities/20041013_6 (in English)

Research Programme Physics and the Built Environment at the Technical University Eindhoven, The Netherlands
http://w3.bwk.tue.nl/nl/onderzoek/onderzoeksprogramma_phbe/ (in English)

Interfaculty Environmental Science Department at University of Amsterdam, The Netherlands
http://www.ivam.uva.nl (in Dutch and in English)

Delft University of Technology, Department of Architecture, Urban Design & Environment
http://www.som.tudelft.nl *(in Dutch)*

ECN: Energy Research Centre of the Netherlands
http://www.ecn.nl/en/ *(In Dutch and in English)*

Consultancies, Organisations, and Projects:
http://www.otterwasser.de *(in German and in English)*
http://www.flintenbreite.de *(in German)*
http://www.zonneterp.nl/english/index_uk.html *(In Dutch and in English)*
http://themas.stowa.nl/Themas/Projects.aspx?mID=7216&rID=1006&aID=1639 *(In Dutch and in English)*
http://www.recyhouse.be/ *(in Dutch, in French, and in English)*
http://www.kringbouw.nl/eng/menu1/menu.php *(In Dutch and in English)*
http://www.sveweb.nl *(In Dutch)*
http://www.agrodome.nl *(In Dutch and in English)*
http://www.rau.eu/site/index_php/Menu/980/pntRef/7/pntScd/d/RAU+WINS +WORLD+BRICK+AWARD+2007.html.html (In Dutch and in English)
http://www.roadenergysystems.nl/ *(In Dutch)*
http://www.cees-bakker.nl/home.php?ID=19 *(In Dutch, in Spanish, and in English)*
http://www.eva-lanxmeer.nl *(in Dutch)*
http://www.iea-shc.org/task23/instruments.htm *(In English)*
http://www.arch.umanitoba.ca/vanvliet/sustainable/cases/ecolonia/ecoindx.htm *(In English)*
http://www.eaue.de/winuwd/57.htm *(In English)*
http://www.hollandsolar.nl/zonnestroom/ *(in Dutch)*
http://www.bear.nl *(In English)*
http://www.smartarchitecture.org *(In English)*
http://www.iea-pvps.org/cases/nld_01.htm *(In English)*

About the editor and the contributors:

Ronald Rovers
Ronald Rovers is Associate Professor at Wageningen University and Research Centre (WUR) and a member of the Urban Environment Management Group, specialized in sustainable building. He is the director of the Sustainable Building Support Centre, an intermediate organisation which contributes to the promotion and development of sustainable building through study tours, workshops, and consultancy. He is vice director of iiSBE, international initiative for a Sustainable Built Environment.

Frank Klinckenberg
Frank Klinckenberg works as a consultant, specialised in policy development and market regulation. As such, Klinckenberg has worked on projects related to energy and sustainable development for the Dutch and British governments, the United Nations Development Programme, the International Energy Agency, the Climate Technology Initiative, the Dutch national energy agency, industry associations and other governmental bodies.

Piet Heijnen
Piet Heijnen is senior advisor at Senternovem, the agency for energy and environment at the Ministry of Economic Affairs. He is specialized in normalisation and regulation, involved with the development and implementation of national and international energy standards (CEN/EPBD), concerned with the development of building and installations techniques (long term research and demonstration) to achieve zero energy buildings, as well as health aspects of the built environment. He is also a member of the Executive Committee of the Implementing Agreement Energy Conservation in Buildings and Community Systems Programme of the IEA.

Martin de Wit
Martin de Wit is Professor of Building Physics at the Eindhoven University of Technology. His research focuses on physical performance of buildings in relation to human comfort and energy performance, heat, humidity and wind.

Mieke Weterings
Mieke Weterings works as an advisor on health aspects of urban planning and sustainable building, for the Environmental Health Office of Rotterdam Municipality. For this project, she contributed especially on the issues of indoor and outdoor air quality, thermal comfort and user-friendliness.

Adriaan Mels
Adriaan Mels works as Associate Professor at the Urban Environment Group of Wageningen University and is also affiliated to the Lettinga Associates Foundation. Mels is specialised in urban water management and participates in development of new concepts for wastewater treatment, especially decentralised sanitation and reuse.

Frans de Haas
Frans de Haas has been involved in sustainable building since its first conception in the Netherlands. With his current office, de Haas & Partners, he focuses on an integral and conceptual approach in the housing and office sector, for both new buildings and renovation, as well as translating this to market strategies.

Martin Mooij
Martin Mooij works at Ecofys, an influential international consultancy on energy and climate change and is educated as an architect at Delft University of Technology. In his work, Mooij focuses on the development and realisation of new concepts for the integration of energy efficiency and sustainable energy in the built environment, in an integral approach including urban planning, energy-infrastructure and buildings, both for housing and commercial buildings, and for new and existing sites.

Kees Duijvestein
Kees Duijvestein is Professor in Environmental Design at the Faculty of Architecture at the Delft University of Technology and strategic advisor for BuildDesk in Delft. Duijvestein stood at the cradle of sustainable building initiatives in the Netherlands and has developed various methods and tools for implementing them. Apart from his academic involvement, Duijvestein acts on various advisory boards and founded BOOM consultants, research and design in environmental urban design.

Ger de Vries
Ger de Vries is managing director, researcher and consultant at V&L Consultants in Rotterdam. He is involved in research and consultancy in the field of sustainable and energy-efficient building and living, the sustainable development of the built environment and trends in environmentally-aware innovations in housing, buildings and the construction industry.
He is Editor of the building journal BouwIQ and a research associate in Environmental Design at the Faculty of Architecture at the Delft University of Technology,.

Tjerk Reijenga
Tjerk Reijenga is architect and principal of BEAR Architecten, an office in sustainable design and planning, focussing on bio climatic architecture. Reijenga is Editor of Sustainable Building International and visiting lecturer in Environmental Building and Design at the Hogeschool Amsterdam.